Bishopthorpe Palace

An Architectural History

With Best Wishes from
Eric and Olive

i

Acknowledgements

We are greatly indebted to Lord Blanch and Lord Coggan, Archbishops of York, and to their families for allowing us access to their home; also to the Church Commissioners for England.

The photograph of The Archbishop of York, Lord Blanch of Bishopthorpe, is reproduced by courtesy of *The Yorkshire Evening Press* and *Gazette & Herald,* York.

The other photographs are reproduced by kind permission of the Royal Commission on Historical Monuments (England), unless otherwise stated.

The River View on page 80 is reproduced by kind permission of Mr. Philip Irving of Hills Boatyard, York.

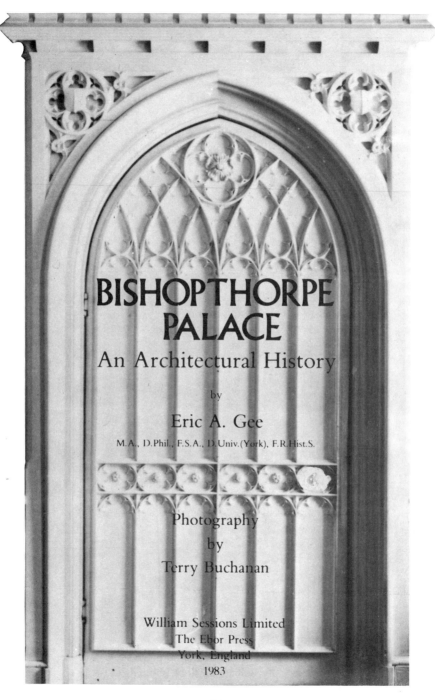

BISHOPTHORPE PALACE

An Architectural History

by

Eric A. Gee

M.A., D.Phil., F.S.A., D.Univ.(York), F.R.Hist.S.

Photography

by

Terry Buchanan

William Sessions Limited
The Ebor Press
York, England
1983

First Published in 1983
ISBN 0 900657 84 7

Printed in Bembo Typeface
by William Sessions Limited,
The Ebor Press, York, England.

LORD BLANCH OF BISHOPTHORPE
Archbishop of York
1975–1983

Foreword

by The Archbishop of York, Primate of England and Metropolitan
Lord Blanch of Bishopthorpe

Dr. Eric Gee has put us all greatly in his debt with this handsome book about Bishopthorpe Palace. My wife and I who have lived in this house for nearly nine years have cause to be grateful for the patient unobtrusive work which Dr. Gee has done in assembling the photographic and descriptive material you will find here. Specialists will value this unique contribution to architectural studies. Local historians will have an unrivalled source of information which could influence their views of domestic architecture elsewhere in the country. Visitors with this book in their hand will be able to understand the various stages through which the house has passed, which they would hardly understand otherwise. And they who have to be content with seeing the house from afar will nevertheless be able to enjoy the visual pleasures of one of the great houses of Yorkshire. May I also pay tribute to Terry Buchanan for the photographs, to Olive Gee and Daphne Wood and to the publishers for the detailed work they have done in bringing this ambitious project to completion. Future occupants of this house will have good cause to be grateful to them all.

Bishopthorpe
York
25th July 1983

Stuart Ebor:

Bishops and Archbishops of York

1 Paulinus, 627-633
2 Chad (Ceadda), 664-669
3 Wilfrid I (St. Wilfrid), 669-677
4 Bosa, 678-705
5 John (St. John of Beverley), 705-
6 Wilfrid II, 718-732
7 Egbert, 735-766
8 Ethelbert, 767-780
9 Eanbald I, 780-796
10 Eanbald II, 796-808
11 Wulfsige, 808-837
12 Wigmund, 837-854
13 Wulfhere, 854-900
14 Ethelbald, 900-
15 Hrotheweard (or Lodeward), 904-931
16 Wulfstan I, 931-956
17 Oskytel, 958-971
18 Edwald (or Ethelwold), 971
19 Oswald, 972-992
20 Ealdulf (Abbot of Peterborough), 992-1002
21 Wulfstan II, 1003-1023
22 Aelfric Puttoc, 1023-1051
23 Cynesige, 1051-1060
24 Ealdred, 1061-1069
25 Thomas I, 1070-1100
26 Gerard, 1101-1108
27 Thomas II, 1109-1114
28 Thurstan, 1119-1140
29 William Fitzherbert, 1143-1147 and 1154
30 Henry Murdac, 1147-1153
    William Fitzherbert
31 Roger of Pont-L'Eveque, 1154-1181
32 Geoffrey Plantagenet, 1181-1191
33 Walter de Grey, 1215-1255
34 Sewal de Bovill, 1256-1258
35 Godfrey of Ludham (or Kineton) 1258-1265
36 Walter Giffard, 1265-1279
37 William Wickwane, 1279-1285
38 John le Romeyn (Romanus). 1286-1296
39 Henry of Newark, 1298-1299
40 Thomas of Corbridge, 1300-1304
41 William Greenfield, 1306-1316
42 William of Melton, 1317-1340
43 William le Zouche, 1342-1352
44 John of Thoresby, 1352-1373
45 Alexander Neville, 1374-1388
46 Thomas Arundel 1388-1396
47 Robert Waldby, 1396-1398
48 Richard le Scrope, 1398-1407
49 Henry Bowet, 1407-1423
50 John Kempe, 1425-1452
51 William Booth, 1452-1464
52 George Neville, 1465-1476
53 Lawrence Booth, 1476-1480
54 Thomas Rotherham (or Scott) 1480-1500
55 Thomas Savage, 1501-1507
56 Christopher Bainbridge, 1508-1514
57 Thomas Wolsey, 1514-1530
58 Edward Lee, 1531-1544
59 Robert Holgate, 1545-1554
60 Nicholas Heath, 1555-1560
61 Thomas Young, 1561-1568
62 Edmund Grindal, 1570-1576
63 Edwin Sandys, 1577-1588
64 John Piers, 1589-1594
65 Matthew Hutton, 1595-1606
66 Tobias Matthew, 1606-1628
67 George Monteigne, 1628
68 Samuel Harsnett, 1628-1631
69 Richard Neile, 1632-1640
70 John Williams, 1641-1650
71 Accepted Frewen, 1660-1664
72 Richard Sterne, 1664-1683
73 John Dolben, 1683-1686
74 Thomas Lamplugh, 1688-1691
75 John Sharp, 1691-1714
76 Sir William Dawes, 1714-1724
77 Lancelot Blackburne, 1724-1743
78 Thomas Herring, 1743-1747
79 Matthew Hutton 1747-1757
80 John Gilbert, 1757-1761
81 Robert Hay Drummond, 1761-1776
82 William Markham, 1777-1807
83 Edward Venables Vernon (afterwards Harcourt), 1807-1847
84 Thomas Musgrave, 1847-1860
85 Charles Thomas Longley, 1860-1862
86 William Thomson, 1862-1890
87 William Connor Magee, 1890-1891
88 William Dalrymple Maclagan, 1891-1908
89 Cosmo Gordon Lang, 1908-1928
90 William Temple, 1929-1942
91 Cyril Forster Garbett, 1942-1955
92 Arthur Michael Ramsey, 1956-1961
93 Frederick Donald Coggan, 1961-1974
94 Stuart Yarworth Blanch, 1975-1983
95 John Stapylton Habgood, 1983-

Contents

Illustrations

Introduction

The Archbishop's Palace at Bishopthorpe is built on slightly rising ground in an attractive position by the river Ouse, some three miles from York. As the river has always been liable to severe flooding, the main rooms of the early house were built on a semi-basement or undercroft. This was totally inundated in January 1982 cutting off light, heat and telephone services in the house; but the later north range is on the higher land so its ground floor shades into the first floor of the medieval house. Because of this discrepancy and owing to the complicated development of the buildings, it has seemed most logical to describe the whole of the exteriors first, starting at the southern corner of the east (river) front and working round in an anti-clockwise direction. The interiors have been examined within each range, starting with the chapel at the upper end, the great hall in the centre and the services at the lower (northern) end of the medieval house.

In the Middle Ages the Archbishop owned a series of manors which supplied him with a large part of his income. Holding the rank of Duke (which is why he is still addressed as 'Your Grace') he was expected to live in great state with an impressive retinue, and would progress from one to the other of his houses at Sherburn-in-Elmet, Reste, Cawood, York and Bishopthorpe, etc., like all great feudal magnates. Over the centuries the other houses were abandoned, chiefly for economic reasons, and most of them destroyed; Bishopthorpe, within easy reach of York but far enough away from the hurly-burly of the great city to ensure a modicum of peace and privacy, has become the sole residence of the Archbishop of York.

Much of the charm of the Palace lies in its infinite variety born of countless additions and adaptations by succeeding prelates: so the eye roves from medieval magnesian limestone to seventeenth-century rusticated brick, to late medieval diaper work and on to the beautifully finished eighteenth-century stone Gothick front; while inside it seems that each new room one enters was built in a different style from the last. The roofs too are varied, most are of plain tile, but slate was introduced by Thomas Atkinson on his Gothick Revival block, the chapel now has tile on the south side and slate on the north side, and the Gothick gateway is roofed with lead. (Throughout this study the spelling *Gothic* is used for the original medieval style while *Gothick* is used for the romantic revival style of the eighteenth century – as the Georgian author Batty Langley spelt it in his books.)

Historical Development

Archbishop Walter de Grey (1215-55) bought the village of Thorpe St. Andrew from Kirkstall Abbey with his own money and appropriated it to the See of York,[1] granting it to the Dean and Chapter in such a way as to ensure continuity and prevent the King obtaining it at each vacancy.[2] There was a twelfth-century manor house on the site which was demolished in 1241, some of its diagonally-axed masonry being re-used in the undercroft. Then the chapel was built with a chantry founded for the souls of King John and all the faithful deceased;[3] in a grant of 18th June 1255 providing for a chaplain for this chantry[4] there are also references to the buildings, gardens and a fishpond made by the archbishop. The chapel and much of the undercroft (1250-5) are built of magnesian limestone from Thevesdale and bear many of the masons' marks which appear on the south transept of York cathedral, while Gilbert de Corbridge, carpenter (men. 1226-48) was rewarded for good service to the archbishop. By January 1316 the village had become known as Bishopthorpe.[5]

The original house consisted of a great hall with a chapel at right-angles to the upper end, and offices with the archbishop's rooms above them at the lower end (as at the first Bishop's Palace at Lincoln and the early arrangement at Dartington Hall, Devon.)[6] In 1364-5 Archbishop John de Thoresby (1352-73) added a new chamber (presumably at the lower end)[7] and in 1383 a visit by Richard II entailed work by masons and carpenters.[8] In c. 1480 Archbishop Rotherham, alias Scott (1480-1500) added the north range, which more than doubled the accommodation. This range is of red brick with diaper in vitrified brick, like contemporary work at the house of the Abbot of St. Mary's Abbey, York, being built in 1483 et seq.[9] In c. 1500 the chapel was given a new east window with five uncusped lights which was removed by Ewan Christian in 1892.

There was a serious attempt by Queen Elizabeth to take the Palace for the Council of the North in 1577, but Archbishop Sandys' protests were successful and the scheme was abandoned.[10] On the 10th March 1647, during the Commonwealth, the Palace was sold for £567 to Colonel Walter White who built two wings on the south side of the north range. He lived there until the Restoration,[11] when it reverted to the church. The palace was in considerable disrepair in 1660 when Archbishop Accepted Frewen (1660-64) took up residence. He rebuilt the great hall with attractive walls of rusticated brick and pilasters at intervals, and gave it an

2

ornate plaster ceiling with his arms (*ermine* four bars *azure* and in chief a demi-lion rampant issuing *proper*) above the fireplace. He fitted rooms above the hall, restored the chapel and gave it a pulpit and high pews inscribed A.F. 1662.[12] However by 31st March 1687 the Palace was again in bad repair, hangings in the chapel were damaged and the Dean and Chapter were ordered to put it right.[13]

Archbishop William Dawes (1714-24) altered the hall and dining room in *c.* 1720[14] and Archbishop John Gilbert (1757-61) altered the windows in the great hall and laid a floor with Roche Abbey stone and black marble.[15] An enriched coved ceiling on the first floor of the north range (over a vanished staircase) is of this date and perhaps by John Carr. In 1743 Thomas Herring, nephew of Archbishop Thomas Herring (1743-7), wrote about the Palace 'Upon the whole it is a most agreeable House and pleases me better than if it had been designed by Lord Burlington or any other genius of the Age.'[16] In 1761-3 Peter Atkinson I, partner of John Carr, built quadrangular stables in a classical style[17] but it was Thomas Atkinson (not related to Peter Atkinson) who built the gateway in 1763-65 and extensive buildings to the west of the main range, all in a romantic Gothick style, for Archbishop Drummond[18] using some stone from Cawood castle.

Archbishop Vernon Harcourt (1807-47) was responsible for important building work at Bishopthorpe. This Regency work with its segmental arches is unlike that of York architects and may have been designed by Sir Robert Smirke, for he restored the eastern arm of York Minster after the fire of 1829, and restored Newnham Park, Oxfordshire, for the Archbishop in 1834. Rooms were put above the chapel and a large block was added to the north-west side of the north range towards the garden [19] in 1835. In about 1840 when the ceiling of the great hall was declared unsafe it was strengthened by iron girders and secured by iron clamps and the rooms above were dismantled.[20] Gas from York was brought to Bishopthorpe in 1867.

There were extensive alterations for Archbishop MacLagan (1891-1908) by Messrs. James Demaine and Walter Brierley, for which a full set of plans are in the lower hall.[21] In 1894 a large room, 48 feet long by 21½ feet wide, was built in part of Mulberry Yard[22] and was used for the first time on 10th July 1894;[23] but this was removed during Dr. Garbett's term of office 1952. The chapel was restored by Ewan Christian in 1892 and reopened in June that year.[24]

The house had reached its maximum extent by 1900. Since then successive archbishops have made it more efficient by designating separate areas for personal apartments, public rooms for the necessary entertainment of dignitaries, and working accommodation for the chaplains and secretariat who help with the increasing administrative work.[25] In 1922 rooms were named after archbishops, under the direction of W. D. Caröe, which greatly aids identification. Electric light was installed for Archbishop Temple (1929-42). In 1965 the staircase in the gallery leading to the dismantled rooms above the great hall was removed. In 1970 there were repairs to the Palace and Lodge by Messrs. Anelay, contractors, under the direction of R. G. Wood, chief architect to the Church Commissioners.[26] The north range was altered in 1972-3 by Victor Brown, architect to the Commissioners, to improve and reduce the size of the Archbishop's residence, leaving the remainder of the range for other church uses.[27]

A very good account of the glass at Bishopthorpe has been produced by Peter Gibson in *The Noble City of York* (York 1972) p.211-213; the remarkable series of portraits of the archbishops of York which hang in the house have been listed and annotated by John Ingamells in *A Catalogue of Portraits at Bishopthorpe Palace* (York 1972).

Footnotes

[1] Chronica Monasterij de Melsa (Rolls Series no 43) 125.
[2] Bishopthorpe II, 19; Bishopthorpe III, 9.
[3] Bishopthorpe II, 19; Bishopthorpe III, 7.
[4] Close Rolls 1254-1256, 100.
[5] Close Rolls 1313-18, 259-60.
[6] T. Buchanan and E. Gee. Bishopthorpe Palace, Residence of the Archbishops of York (York 1983), 2.
[7] Thoresby Register fol. 321v; 322r; 322v.
[8] *Country Life* 14. Sept. 1961.
[9] Browne Willis, *Survey of Cathedrals,* I, (London 1742) quoting Torre.
[10] Calendar of State Papers Domestic 1577-8, 537-8.
[11] Drake, *Eboracum* (1736) 383.
[12] Bishopthorpe III, 13.
[13] Calendar of Treasury Books 1685-89, Part III, 1383.
[14] Drake, ut supra, 383.
[15] J. R. Keble, *History of Bishopthorpe* (Leeds 1905) 82.
[16] Bishopthorpe III, 25, quoting Nicholas, *Literary Anecdotes*.
[17] J. W. Knowles, MSS in York Reference Library, 9 & 11.
[18] Ann Ward, *History and Antiquities of York* (York 1785) III, 79.
[19] Bishopthorpe III, 19.
[20] Bishopthorpe III, 31.
[21] Bishopthorpe III, 56.
[22] Bishopthorpe III, 67.
[23] Bishopthorpe IV, 17.
[24] Bishopthorpe III, 59; Bishopthorpe IV, 4.
[25] T. Buchanan and E. Gee ut Supra. 2.
[26] Stapleton, Pace and Day, *A Skilful Master Builder.* (York 1975) 71.
[27] Notes by Mrs. Coggan. Mr. Brown kindly provided the author with a full set of plans.

LOCATION MAP

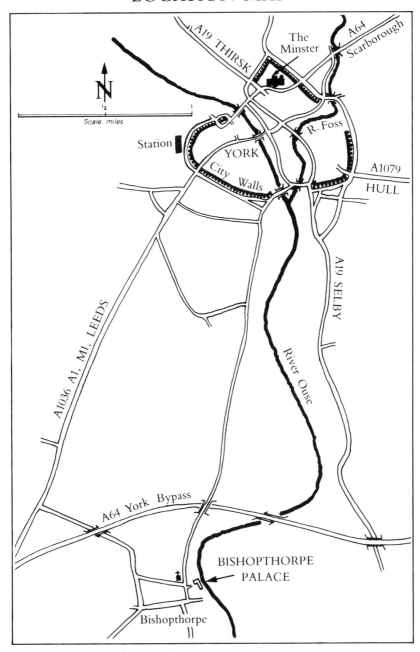

PLANS

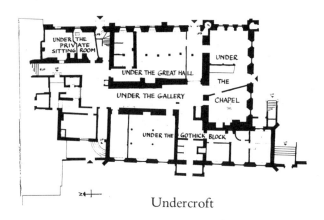

Undercroft

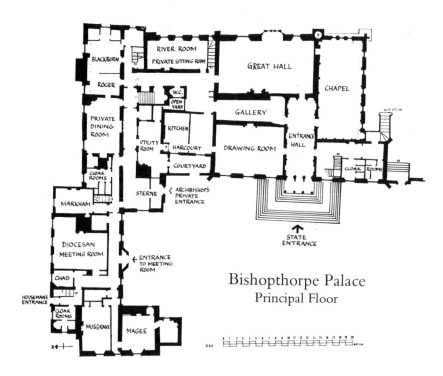

Bishopthorpe Palace
Principal Floor

6

PLANS

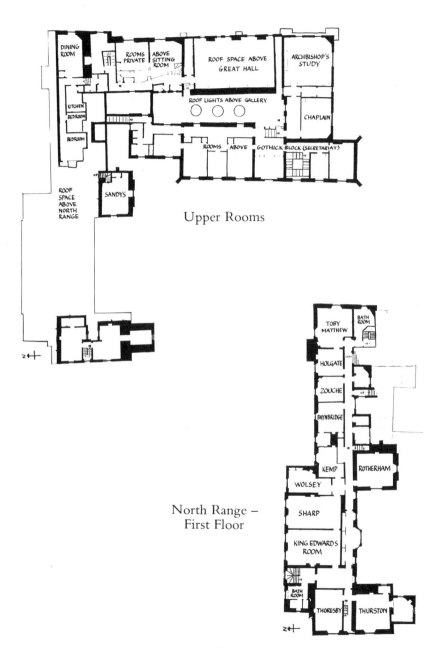

DINING ROOM · **ROOMS PRIVATE** · **ABOVE SITTING ROOM** · **ROOF SPACE ABOVE GREAT HALL** · **ARCHBISHOP'S STUDY** · **ROOF LIGHTS ABOVE GALLERY** · **KITCHEN** · **BEDROOM** · **BEDROOM** · **CHAPLAIN** · **ROOMS ABOVE** · **GOTHICK BLOCK (SECRETARIAT)** · **ROOF SPACE ABOVE NORTH RANGE** · **SANDYS**

Upper Rooms

North Range –
First Floor

TOBY MATTHEW · **BATH ROOM** · **HOLGATE** · **ZOUCHE** · **BAYNBRIDGE** · **KEMP** · **ROTHERHAM** · **WOLSEY** · **SHARP** · **KING EDWARDS ROOM** · **BATH ROOM** · **THORESBY** · **THURSTON**

Architectural Description

The house consists of a medieval main range running north to south and parallel to the river, with a large addition of 1766-9 on its west side. At the north end of the main range and facing the garden is a late medieval range of *c*. 1480, running east to west, with a Regency block of 1835 added to the north-west of the north front and two blocks of *c*. 1650 built against the south side.

Exteriors

The East Front shows most of the phases of development of the whole house. The block at the south end is the east wall of the **chapel** (page 50) and at the bottom it has a low square projection which was a garderobe, weathering into buttresses above with a modern shouldered headed doorway in its south face. The main east face is of good ashlar and in the centre three blocked windows represent original lancets, but are not old in their present form. To the north is a large oblong projection containing a newel stair, intact for the full height of the chapel, with a small oblong light to the undercroft and a gable with moulded coping at the top. At first floor level there are thirteenth-century buttresses above the garderobe, like that on the newel, and on the inner side of these are round shafts with water-holding bases but no capitals. Three lancets by Ewan Christian (1892) replaced an east window of *c*. 1500. The third stage of 1835 has a pedimental gable and chimney, and two hung-sash windows with four-centred heads and chamfered reveals.

The **hall range** (page 51) is to the north. At its south end, against the chapel newel stair, is a remnant of stone walling showing the character of the thirteenth-century elevation, with a string course at the top of the undercroft level and a second string which would have risen over the main hall lancets, and a piece of the water table showing the top of the original hall. At the north end is a pilaster buttress which proves that Archbishop Frewen's remodelling is the same height as the thirteenth-century hall. At undercroft level, which is all of excellent thirteenth-century ashlar, is a large segmental-headed doorway with a fanlight with intersecting tracery of 1830-40; an original early thirteenth-century lancet of two chamfered orders with deep weathering; a buttress holding an oriel above (perhaps of seventeenth century date); an original lancet and two blocked lancets (there may have been six lancets here at first). The main floor is of rusticated brick and has a waterhead with 'A.F. 1662'. There are four pilasters at intervals, square in plan with moulded brick capitals and bases on corbels. There are string courses between these capitals and bases and under the capital is a stucco band with dentils. In the wall between the pilasters are tall wooden windows, one with a mullion and transome remodelled in 1758-60, a three-sided oriel of much the same form supported on the buttress and with a tiled roof, and a window with two mullions and a transome. The rusticated walling finishes in a straight line beyond the last pilaster to the north. Above is an area of later plain brick with in it six hung-sash windows under a two-brick band; and above again are three tumbled gables each with a blocked window, a flat section at the top and low walls on either side hiding the valley. There is a boldly projecting ashlar buttress at the north end of the hall block, with a chamfered base, a moulded string at the top of the undercroft and a weathering at the top of the original hall.

A **section of ashlar to the north** again (page 51) is in the same plane as the hall undercroft. In this ashlar is a doorway with two-centred head (1891-2), a window in a recess of the same shape and with large panes, and a second similar window but with hung sashes and small panes (early nineteenth century); all three openings represent lights to the buttery, pantry and passage of 1364-5. The archbishop's accommodation above it on the first floor has a small light to the inserted staircase and three large windows with two-centred heads and hollow chamfered reveals; probably these each had a mullion and two cinquefoiled lights above and below a transome, but they now have hung-sashes with intersecting glazing bars at the top. In the second floor are two square-headed windows each with labels and hung-sashes; the adjacent water heads are dated 1848 and the tiled roof over this section runs north to south. There is another broad buttress to the north with boldly weathered base and top with on it a smaller two-stage buttress showing the top of Thoresby's addition.

A large **block at the north end** projects (page 51) and consists of two parts, one perhaps representing the thirteenth-century kitchen and the other a late fifteenth-century kitchen at the end of Archbishop Rotherham's added north range. The one part has a modern hung-sash window inserted in April 1972 and above it is the window from which it was copied (eighteenth century), with a section of string course to its south representing the top of the original building. At the top is a brick gable with a relatively modern hung sash window. The other part is of ashlar with a chamfered plinth and a brick gable at the top, all of c. 1480, and each floor is lit with a square-headed hung-sash window with moulded hood mould.

The North Range
The whole of this block built c. 1480 remains with some additions and modifications. The **north front** is in two planes for the western half sets forward strongly; remnants of later colour wash are visible along all this front.

The **eastern part** (page 52) was built of brick in the late fifteenth century, with good ashlar quoins at the north-east corner and no divisions between the storeys. A large square chimney breast with a chamfered stone plinth projects and has stone quoins with late tooling on the east side and medieval tooling on the west; it incorporates a large chimney, with diagonal sections supported on moulded brick corbels, of *c.* 1500, above which is an oblong addition of the seventeenth century, heightened again in the early nineteenth century and topped with five chimney pots. To the east of this breast the wall has a chamfered stone plinth and the remains of diaper in vitrified bricks. The lower window was inserted in 1972 and the upper one has an ashlar surround and early hung-sashes with heavy glazing bars (*c.* 1750). The wall has been heightened and has a moulded brick coping.

To the west of the chimney breast the wall is of the same character with remnants of diaper, but with a brick plinth and a relatively modern parapet. At ground floor level the first window is of eighteenth-century type but has been extended down in 1972 to the plinth; its top sash has broad glazing bars (*c.* 1750) but the lower one is modern. A fall pipe to the west is round with opposed fleurs-de-lis on the astragals and a shaped waterhead set at the proper water table level. The second and third windows are like the first but between them is a wide stretch of wall with 'ragged joints' indicating the position of a large earlier window. A small light to the west has hollow chamfered brick jambs and a diagonally placed iron stanchion (*c.* 1480), and beyond two modern fall pipes, another eighteenth-century window has been extended down to the plinth. At first floor level the first and third windows have hung-sashes of early nineteenth-century form, while the second and fourth are narrower with earlier hung-sashes; between them is plenty of evidence for the earlier broader mullioned windows. The roof running east to west is of ordinary clay tiles and has a chimney breast to west of centre of *c.* 1830 with four modern pots.

The **western part of the north front** projects (*c.* 1830) (page 52) and is of large good-quality buff brick, once whitewashed. It is symmetrically designed with seven bays with moulded stone copings and has two gables, between slightly recessed bays, at either side. The east face of this block has two segmental-headed blocked windows; on the north face the windows are all alike, with plain ashlar surround and stone sill, the hung-sashes have thin glazing bars and crown glass. In the gables are bulls-eye windows with a plain stone surround and bricks set on edge. A doorway in the place of the sixth window from the east has a plain stone surround, simple moulded cornice, segmental fanlight and a door with six fielded panels. There are similar segmental-headed recesses in the return at the west end but each has in it a small modern light. The **last bay on the north front** is medieval, with a little diaper, a good ashlar quoin and a late parapet.

The **west end of the north range** (page 53), with a contemporary block to its south, are all of *c.* 1480 and are of brick with a lot of diaper work; above a high-set plinth with a chamfered stone top member, it has two gables and ashlar quoins but no string courses. The ground floor has two windows with ashlar surround and pairs of hung-sashes with thin glazing bars divided by a wooden upright, and between them a narrower window of much the same date. At first floor level are two larger windows (in the blockings of earlier ones) with paired hung-sashes and smaller panes, and a central window like the narrower one below. There is excellent diaper in the northern gable and less in the southern one; both have late windows inserted and both have later heightening, the valley between being closed with a parapet of two dates topped with a moulded stone coping.

The **south front of the north range** (page 53) is built against the main range at the east end where it is covered by later buildings; otherwise this 1480 building has projecting blocks at either end.

The **south east block** has a large chimney breast on its east side and a projecting centre on its south side with stone quoins and plinth as before. In 1972 a doorway was inserted with stone surround and a glazed door. At first floor level there is a late eighteenth-century hung-sash window and the attic is lit by a small casement light in a gable with stone copings. There is a section of plain walling on either side of the projection. In the south-west angle is an attractive lead waterhead with fluted bowl with cornice and paterae below. The west side is like Colonel White's block of *c.* 1650 to the south-west and the gable has been heightened. Ground and first floors each have pairs of hung-sash windows with stone surrounds and sills, and in the west gable is a sliding sash window with stone surround and sill.

The **main south face of the north range** is symmetrical with a bay window of magnesian limestone in the centre (*c.* 1500). In the middle of the outer face of this bay at ground floor level is an inserted doorway, but the earlier jambs of the window show on either side, also an indication of the sill level. In each oblique face is a tall light blocked with eighteenth-century ashlar. Above the door are two hung-sash windows with their outer jambs formed by the original mullions, while the oblique sides have hung-sash windows, one pane wide, with original jambs and later lintels of buff stone. The roof of the bay is formed of five chamfered steps of ashlar. On either side of the bay are two hung-sash windows to ground and first floor with a section of diaper showing in the walling. The front is finished with a tall brick parapet of *c.* 1830 with stone coping.

The **south-west block** (page 53) is in two planes; at the north end is a large gabled projection which has at the centre a chimney breast of *c.* 1480 with a chamfered plinth of magnesian limestone, four courses of ashlar and, above this, brick walling with excellent diaper; at the top is the remnant of a sixteenth-century chimney like that at the east end of the

11

north face of this range. This chimney breast originally projected, but to its north is an infill of brick on a chamfered plinth of stone (eighteenth century), and to the south is a wall with limestone quoins with, at ground level, an eighteenth-century hung-sash window – its north jamb being cut into the medieval chimney – and above it is a smaller hung-sash window. The south face of the gabled projection is of redder brick than the medieval part and there is a straight joint to the west. The gable has an added slope up to a relatively modern chimney breast. At the south end is the block added by Colonel White in c. 1650 and there is evidence for mullioned windows in both floors. At the bottom is an eighteenth-century hung-sash window to the north of centre. The south end of the block has stone quoins and the first floor is lit by a mid-eighteenth-century hung-sash window with heavy glazing bars, probably in the blocking of an earlier window, and there is a casement in the gable. The west side has no features.

The West Front

There is a **small courtyard** between the north east block which is added on the south side of the north range, and the late eighteenth-century block added to the west of the main range. It has on the west side a curtain wall of good ashlar with a moulded parapet and plinth; in this is a doorway with continuous moulded reveals and a segmental head beneath an ogee crocketted gable with finial; it has weathered label stops, cruciform arrow-slits in the spandrels and over the doorway, bold battlements on a moulded string. The door has two trefoiled lights formed by bold mouldings on vertical planks (1766-9).

A range to the east side is of two storeys on an undercroft. The bottom of the wall is rendered and in it is a sliding sash window and a doorway with plain ashlar surround, a segmental head and simple moulded label. The plank door has vertical applied mouldings. The brick ground floor has two hung-sash windows, each with two-centred head and label with hollow chamfered mouldings in brown ashlar, and over the arch is a second arch of plain brick. The top sash has intersecting tracery and small panes (c. 1770) and the lower sash is of Victorian plate glass. The first floor has similar windows and at the top is a battlemented ashlar parapet. The dressings project a little as if for rendering. The north face of the old main west front is of brick with a stuccoed base and there is a big group of modern fall pipes.

The **west front of the Gothick range** of 1766-9 built by Thomas Atkinson (page 54), is of very good regular ashlar and is of two storeys and an undercroft. It is of seven bays with moulded plinth and at the top is a Gothic/Classical hybrid of a parapet, with foliated consoles and moulding under open battlements. The cornice rises over a pediment at the centre, and its bottom member continues across the chord of the pediment. On either side of the porch in the large central bay are three bays. The undercroft windows have square heads, moulded reveals and a moulded label dropping to square returns; they have hung-sashes with large panes and strong glazing bars. Windows covered by the steps have a glazed top, and outside the second, fifth and sixth are slender railings with at the top in each case the crest of Archbishop Drummond (a hand holding a dagger).

Each of the ground floor hung-sash windows has a segmental head and moulded ogee label, with diminutive crockets and a fine large finial. The reveals are like those of the undercroft windows. The top sash has six panes and intersecting tracery with cusps inside the glass; the lower sash has plate glass. Between the windows at the level of the stops is a moulded string course, and at the level of the finials is an ornate band of decoration. Three courses above the band is a moulded string, this produces the same effect as the band and continuous sill of classical houses built by the firm of John Carr, and also by Atkinson himself.

The top storey has similar but less deep windows with original sashes and no cusps; all windows have crocketted labels and finials. In the centre of the first floor an oriel window shown on an engraving of 1773 (page 54) was removed in 1929 by W. D. Caröe, although a segmental strainer arch remains and in the blocking is a window copying the others but with more effective stops (a monster's head with close set eyes and mouth askew, and a man's head with a bendy nose). The bottom element of the cornice steps up over the position of the oriel.

At each end of this front is a diagonal buttress of three orders with a bold plinth at the level of the ground floor window-sills, a set-in just above the decorative band (which carries round the buttress as does the open top parapet) and at the top an eagle with wings spread. The eagle and much of the parapet were restored in 1934-5 by George Milburn of York.

The porch forms a grand canopy three bays wide and one bay deep. On the east side are four responds each with triple shafts, all with foliated capitals, with moulded abacus, roll, neckings and attic bases. On the west side are corresponding free-standing columns of the same form and connected to the responds with iron ties. At each end are two-centred moulded arches with a band of double-cusped decoration. The ogee label has crocketting and a bold finial and in each spandrel is a trefoil and two daggers. At each angle is a square pinnacle with panelled sides and a crocketted top with finial and under these are demi-angels holding shields:– (1) plain; (2) a church, badly weathered; (3) the See of York impaling quarterly 1 & 4 barry wavy of eight [*argent* and *gules*] a scimitar in pale hilt downwards [*or*] 2 & 3 [*azure*] a unicorn salient [*argent*] hoofed and maned [*or*] in a bordure [*or*] charged with demi-thistles impaled with demi-roses (Archbishop Drummond); (4) a human figure; (5) Virgin and child (modern); (6) plain. The original shields are heater shaped, the modern ones are broader and relatively crude. The outer roof of the porch curves inwards, with a band of enrichment on it, to a demi-octagonal head which carried the original oriel window. Inside is a delightful fan vault.

The steps rise in two suites of six steps and four steps from three sides, and there are two iron lamp standards, with octagonal shafts on openwork bases, carrying octagonal lamps.

This Gothick block returns on the south side in ashlar with another diagonal buttress at the south east corner. The east face is of brick and has a porch at the bottom with a segmental opening, above it a modern doorway and at the top a wooden gutter on foliated consoles. The modern staircase in Mulberry Yard was fitted in the time of Archbishop Cosmo Lang (1909-28)

We complete the circuit of the exterior with the **south wall of the chapel range** (page 50). This is of three stages, the bottom two of *c.* 1250 and of magnesian limestone, the top one of *c.* 1830 and of buff stone. At the east end is a square projection with the remains of a chamfered plinth, weathering back, and on the weathering a buttress to each face of the angle. In the south face is a shouldered-headed doorway with continuous hollow chamfered reveals (*c.* 1830); the door is of vertical planks with simple applied mouldings. The main south wall has four windows, modern in their present form, with two chamfered orders, flattened head and strong stancheons. In the middle is a doorway with flattened head and chamfered orders, a Gothick fanlight and two oak doors.

Above this undercroft stage the wall sets-in above a deeply moulded string and here the chapel wall is original with five lancets equally spaced, each with a two-centred head and of two chamfered orders; a moulded label continues across at springing level to form a string course. At the top is a bold string course of half-dogtooth decoration like that at York Cathedral.

The top storey, added by Archbishop Vernon Harcourt, has long stones of buff ashlar with iron cramps in the mortar joints. At the top is a simple battlemented parapet. In the centre is a narrow hung sash window with two-centred head, plain chamfered reveals and simple moulded label. On either side is a large square-headed window with three lights and high transome and toggled head.

Interior of the Main Range

The **Main Range** has a thirteenth-century undercroft, with above it the chapel of 1241 to the south, the great hall, remodelled in 1660-1664 at the centre, and the Archbishop's private sitting room to the north (1364-5 and later).

The Undercroft

The undercroft, or basement floor, of the Palace is archaeologically the most important part of the building and consists of the virtually intact bottom storey of the medieval house of 1220-40 (page 55) with additions of 1765-9 by Thomas Atkinson. (Plan page 6.)

The **chapel undercroft** is now divided by a through passage running north to south. The east wall of the eastern part has four openings all with round-headed rere-arches with hollow chamfered reveals. The head of the first lancet is open but the rest is blocked; there are good voussoirs above it. A similar lancet next to it runs down to sill level, which has on it a sink-like slab, and the reveals are slightly splayed; the top is set above the outer surround and the lancet is of nineteenth-century date with a sheet of glass protected by three vertical bars and a horizontal. Next is a similar window cut down to a ground level, with only the top open and the remainder blocked. The fourth opening is a small doorway to a garderobe lit by lancets to the east and south, with a quadripartite vault with hollow chamfered ribs. The roof of the lancets and the web of the vault are of tiles set on edge. There is a modern doorway in the south end. These openings are all close together, the ashlar has mouldings on both sides and there is some make-up in brick. The north and south walls are of ashlar and each has a bold hollow chamfered projecting course at the top which held the original floor of the chapel. In the north wall is an eighteenth-century doorway with segmental head and square brick reveals. In the south wall are two thirteenth-century windows with some brick blocking and sills at the original level. The brick west wall is a later insertion.

The north end of the **passage** has a doorway with on the one side a round head, hollow chamfered reveals and large late voussoirs, and on the other side a segmental head and square reveals. The east wall has a timber grille and the west wall has a doorway with moulded case and early nineteenth-century door. The south wall has a doorway set in an original window opening with a hollow chamfered jamb on the east side.

The third part is now a boiler room but in 1892 it was a laundry. It retains the hollow chamfered projecting course to support the chapel floor to north and south but not to the west. The east wall forms the west wall of the passage. The plastered ashlar north wall has a small doorway with a nineteenth-century door leading to the eighteenth-century passage formed when the Gothick range was added. The ashlar west wall may be of the thirteenth century and has a round-headed recess with brick head, a blocked fireplace, an iron tank set on modern brick, and a high-set lamp recess. The south wall has two modern lancets set in early nineteenth-century rere-arches.

The **great undercroft under the hall** has in the north east corner a wine cellar constructed in brick. The north wall of this is of seventeenth-century brick, but one would expect ashlar so it could encase stone; it abuts ashlar in the east wall, but some modern brick at the top represents the strengthening of the hall floor which is otherwise supported on R.S.J.s. In the thirteenth-century east wall (page 56) is the rere-arch of an opening with segmental head and hollow chamfered jambs, now blocked with seventeenth-century brick. The brick south wall runs into a second rere-arch in the east wall, with ventilation holes in it, and an R.S.J. at the top. In the west wall a doorway had two concentric brick arches making a segmental head on the outside and rebated on the inside. The door is of heavy vertical planks, with horizontals and strap hinges on the inner side, and at the top are two circular ventilation holes with original seventeenth-century iron fittings. The ceiling beams, set on edge, are seventeenth-century and on the north side of the wine cellar there is a shelf consisting of stone flags set at chest height on four chord walls of brick.

The **undercroft otherwise** is of the same width as the great hall above but although the east wall is of *c.* 1230 the character of the west wall is more difficult to define. Much of the north wall is covered by the wine cellar, but a small section of it to the west has a doorway in it of late seventeenth-century date, set in brick with a segmental spandrel under a large flat oak head. To the east of it is rough stone with some brick patching. On the west there is a cut back wall with some brick make-up and beyond is the original wall some two feet six inches thick, retaining some re-used Norman stone and some claw-tooled thirteenth-century stone well toothed into the west wall. Against the west wall is a re-used ceiling beam set on an upright and intended to support the seventeenth-century hall floor above. The thirteenth-century east wall (page 55) is not perfect and at the top are five courses of brick of *c.* 1660 to support the hall floor. There are two thirteenth-century lancets set close together with segmental rere-arches and hollow chamfered reveals, and with brick inserted at the bottom to raise the sills. The third lancet is similar (page 56) but some distance away and all three have masons' marks on them. At the south end a large inserted doorway has the remnant of a thirteenth-century rere-arch near the bottom of its north jamb. The doorway has a large segmental arch and chamfered brick jambs, all plastered; the door fittings are of *c.* 1830. The west wall is medieval and contains Norman and thirteenth-century masonry; at the centre is a brick feature probably supporting the hall fireplace above, but containing a re-used thirteenth-century rere-arch (page 57); there is a large relatively modern opening at the south end. The south wall is thick and chiefly of thirteenth-century date; at its east end is a square-headed opening to a newel stair leading up to the chapel (this was opened up and explored by Archbishop Maclagan and his gardener in 1897); the lower steps are broken and there is a small oblong light to the east. There is a large seventeenth-century doorway with brick jambs and segmental head and beyond and to the west again is the head of a shouldered-headed opening which could represent a window. At the west end of the south wall is a large square-headed doorway with hollow chamfered reveals and blocked with stone.

The **north part of the undercroft,** under the archbishop's private sitting room, consists of a small room formed by various inserted walls. The north wall is of mixed construction with a projecting centre of brick; to its east is a blocked doorway with a wooden lintel and chamfered jambs of narrow brick with wide mortar joints (probably *c.* 1480) and to its west an eighteenth-century cupboard with fielded panels. In the east wall is a medieval window with two-centred head and glazed with small eighteenth-century panes. It has an elegant hollow chamfered rere-arch of 1364-5, of segmental form in good ashlar (page 57); the north jamb of the window has been remodelled with bricks on edge. In the west wall is a doorway formed in the rere-arch of a medieval window, and to its south is a late brick projection with in it a large oven by J. Walker of York (early nineteenth-century). At the top on the east side are both jambs of an early thirteenth-century lancet. The south wall is of brick in two planes, with the east half projecting.

A second room is in much better order than the first one. The north wall may be of late nineteenth-century date as it is built into a fireplace connecting with the early nineteenth-century oven in the other room. A window at the north end of the east wall is not medieval in its present form but it is set into an early thirteenth-century rere-arch not as wide as that in the first room. The projecting north part of the west wall has a deep recess which is part of a fireplace. A doorway to the south has hollow chamfered reveals and segmental head like the original window but the round head of the doorway is set low because of a ceiling on the other side, so it may be later. The door is of heavy vertical planks and has a frame to the passage producing three panels and opens on large strap hinges on hooks (early eighteenth century). The south wall is relatively modern.

To the south of the last room is a lobby with a staircase in it. The brick north wall, with wide white mortar joints could be of seventeenth-century date. The plastered east wall has two lights at the top, and on the south side is the underneath of the nineteenth-century staircase. A doorway in the medieval west wall has two continuous chamfered orders, the outer one hollow chamfered, and on the inner side is a deep rere-arch with segmental head and hollow chamfered reveals. The plastered south wall runs into the rere-arch of the doorway on its south side.

To the west of the rooms is a long passage running north and south. The north wall has a door with six fielded panels set high on three steps. The plastered east wall is of medieval ashlar and has in it three doorways, some inserted into windows. The west wall has a square-headed doorway leading to a lobby on the west. This narrow part of the range could have embodied a medieval buttery and pantry with the passage leading to a kitchen beyond and to the north.

The **undercroft of the block of 1766-9** provided better circulation for the medieval undercroft, and some new staff rooms. At the northern end of this later complex is a yard with buildings of mid-eighteenth-century date and later. A long **passage** of varying widths runs north to south on the west of the medieval range then turns round the chapel undercroft. The thin plastered north wall of the passage has in it a hung-sash window with segmental head, an upper sash of four panes, a lower one of eight panes, and broad ovolo moulded glazing bars of *c.* 1750. The east wall has an opening to a hall at the south end of a lobby, a thin screen of nineteenth-century date and a large stretch of early walling. The early walling has at its north end some nicely pointed narrow brick on a plinth above some exposed footings (late seventeenth-century) and beyond that some well-coursed ashlar with an early thirteenth-century chamfered plinth. The next part projects slightly and is probably the base of the hall fireplace (seventeenth-century). The last part is lath and plaster with a large flattened-headed archway with chamfered reveals which gave access to the earlier undercroft, the bottom is blocked and in the top is a nineteenth-century window with small panes. The west wall (1766-9) has various openings to the rooms in the Gothick block. There is a large **servants hall,** now divided, with a tank room on its north side, and containing (in 1980) the newel and some balusters with umbrella knops of a destroyed early eighteenth-century staircase once in the gallery. There is a store room with arched roof under the main entrance stairs. The **butler's pantry** is also divided and has a large early nineteenth-century cupboard in the east wall, a fireplace in the centre with two enriched panels on either side and tanks in the hobs. There is a **store** at the south end with a rectangular opening in the north wall, a segmental-headed recess in the east wall, probably a doorway but now containing a small sliding-sash window with very small panes. To its south is a shallow recess with splayed jambs which was probably a window. All these rooms are lit on the west side with hung-sash windows of 1766-9, each with six large panes, thin large glazing bars, plain panelled shutters and a sloping base, and with the head above the ceiling.

Principal Floor
The Chapel

Plan for principal Floor of Palace see page 6.

The chapel is basically the fabric of 1241 which was restored by Archbishop Accepted Frewen in 1662. When the Gothick building was erected by Thomas Atkinson in 1766-9 the west windows of the chapel were blocked and some arcading was removed on the north side. The pews were richly carved and some were of deal; the walls were oil painted a dull blue and the ceiling dark brown. There was a large oak throne for the archbishop on one side and an oak pulpit on the other. The most important restoration in modern times was that by Ewan Christian begun in January 1892. The ceiling was coloured in alternate squares of red and green and two texts (since removed) were painted as a sort of frieze; on the north was *Stituit anima mea ad Deum fortem vivum, quando veniam et apparebo ante faciem Deo.* (PS. xlii, 2); and on the south was *Beati qui lavant stolas suas in sanguine agni. Videbunt faciem eius ad nomen eius in pontibus eorum.* (Rev. xxii, 14 & 4). The floor was lowered ten inches and the east end was put on three steps to give it dignity. The sanctuary was newly paved in polished black and white marble and the old marble pavement in the body of the chapel was relaid. The blue painting of the walls was removed with acid, exposing fine ashlar, and the arcading and the stone bench were restored. The archbishop's throne and the pulpit were removed in April 1896 and were given to Wilfred, eldest son of Archbishop Thomson to be put in the church at Rotherfield, where his brother-in-law Canon Goodwin (who moved to Eastbourne in 1898) was incumbent. The chapel was again restored *c*. 1920 by W. D. Caröe.

Architectural Description
The chapel is virtually all medieval but there is no regular bay system, for the north and south walls differ (page 58). The east wall, of irregular ashlar at the bottom, steps-in at the south end to provide a modern seat supported on two shaped corbels and is associated with an adjacent piscina (1903); a recessed section above the seat is medieval and has a chamfer under the window. In the upper part of the wall are five recesses with elaborately moulded, two-centred arches on simple round freestone shafts with moulded capitals and bases and high round plinths. There are lancets in the second, third and fourth recesses designed by Ewan Christian in 1892 at the request of Archbishop Maclagan. Between the lancets are corbels with moulding corresponding to the adjacent shafts, and with strange fluted bases. High up in the north east corner is a moulded corbel which may have supported the original roof. The present wall face may have been set-forward; a recess slopes out to a low-set shaft which could represent an arrangement like that in Fountains Abbey choir.

The north wall is not like the south one nor does it line up with features in the east wall. In general it has a finely-moulded string course at the top and modern benches at the bottom. There are in sequence a half bay, four large bays, a blocked doorway, a narrow bay and a half bay. Each bay has a tall recess with two-centred arch, chamfered reveals, no imposts and a simple moulded label, but the half-bay has a head with moulded label and a cut away stop. There is a straight joint for much of the height towards the east wall. The first full bay has in it an inserted doorway, rediscovered by Archbishop Magee in 1891/2; it is of very large stones with a two-centred head and continuous reveals with two wave moulds (fourteenth-century) on the south side. The north side of the doorway can be seen in a cupboard formed behind the softwood panelling in the great hall; the rere-arch has a flattened head and chamfered reveals and is set in a great two-centred archway with, on the east, a moulded abacus on a smiling angel with curly hair and small wings folded under his chin. The west side drops to a chamfered respond and a wall bench. The modern oak plank door folds in the centre. The second, third and fourth bays have good modern oak panelling in them. To the west of the fourth bay the label carries across horizontally as a string above the rere-arch of a large blocked doorway with flattened two-centred head, half-octagonal jambs and splayed reveals; this was an external doorway to the chapel from the grounds, and on it is an inscription slab recording the restoration of 1892 by Archbishop William Dalrymple Maclagan. In the next bay is a modern doorway (opened by Archbishop Magee 1891) with segmental chamfered head and square reveals; the jambs look older and one side of the arch on the east has an old stone in it but the west side and the respond standing on a shaped corbel are all modern. There would have been an orthodox bay with a lancet in it beyond the doorway but it has been remade to produce the present shouldered head. Two voussoirs of the original head remain and the walling in the corner is old. In the north-west corner is a shaft with moulded capital and very high plinth like that in the east wall.

Unlike the north wall the south wall is ornate and attractive, with alternating recesses and lancets. The bays each have a bold, moulded, two-centred arch supported on either side by a round, engaged, freestone shaft with moulded capital, moulded water-holding base and a very tall plinth. At the top of the wall is an ornate string and at the bottom a bench. Each lancet has a two-centred head and splayed reveals, with a flattened two-centred rere-arch and chamfered sill. The first bay has a round arch and within this is a large oblong recess with a modern square-headed piscina, with a shaped inner head and bowl on a triple shaft with a moulded cap and base, and the inscription **W** MCMIII **E**. The last bay was blind, but now has a modern round-headed doorway, with a modern plank door. A shaft in the south-west corner has an original capital, base and plinth; on the west side of the top arch is a carved stop of a man with the lower roll of the moulding going into his mouth.

The west wall has five tall blind arches like the east one, with the centre three arches round and the side ones asymmetrical, like some in the choir at Fountains Abbey. The shafts have moulded bell capitals, water-holding bases and very high plinths; the arches and labels are moulded; the walling is of plain ashlar but the bottom is covered with modern panelling, and in the centre three arches are seats for the archbishop and two bishops fitted in 1892. At the top of the wall are oblique lines of moulding which must have been a decorative feature under the original gable.

The roof consists of a flat timber ceiling all properly pegged and is probably *c*. 1500. It has five major moulded tie beams and six minor ones, and five longitudinal moulded ceiling beams. It is painted blue, with gold, green, purple and red on the beams, and the main ties bear central bands composed of chevrons in white, red and black, bordered by stripes of green and gold. In the centre of each panel at the east end are shields bearing alternately a saltire and 'IHS' in Gothic capitals. The floor is of fine limestone flags and black marble. The High Altar is on a step and the sanctuary is two steps above the nave which has a floor of diagonal slabs. There is a large grille at the west end and a step down into the entrance hall.

Chapel Fittings

Altar	Modern. Mrs. William Lefroy (née Claire Peirse, d. 20th Aug. 1907) gave a large oak altar at the restoration of 1892. In the time of Archbishop Coggan (1961-74) the communion table was brought forward and the dorsal curtains were removed. Riddel posts in the chapel, originally carved angels, had been removed in the time of Archbishop Ramsey (1956-61).
Altar rails	Made by Messrs Simpson *c*. 1960.
Aumbry	In north wall. Found in 1920, doors fitted by W. D. Caröe.
Chandeliers	Two; elegant brass chandeliers, on either side of the High Altar.
Crosses	Behind the altar, a very effective blue and red plastic cross with heavy bronze-like base. This modern laminated cross and two candlesticks were designed by Colin Auger of Ampleforth in the time of Archbishop Coggan.
Cushions	Tapestry cushions at the west end, embroidered by Archbishop Donald Coggan (1961-74) and given to the chapel prior to his translation to Canterbury. (1) Arms of the See of York. (2) The See of Durham. (3) The See of Bradford. (4) On a smaller cushion on the Bishop's chair, the See of York.
Font	A medieval mortar set in a piece of oak, found in the kitchen part of the undercroft in 1982, has been placed in the chapel by Archbishop Blanch (1974-83) as a font and used to christen his two grand-children.
Glass	Coats of arms were made by William Peckitt in 1767 and fitted in the east and south windows of the chapel. They were replaced in 1892 and new glass fitted by Charles Eamer Kempe.

Icon	Of St. George; figures in white metal on a brass background with fine enamelled and enriched surround. Given to Archbishop Garbett in 1943 in Moscow.
Monument	In a recess in the north wall to the immediate east of the entrance doorway; a wall monument of alabaster with the arms of Grey of Rotherfield with a mitre on top, for Archbishop Walter de Grey, and at the bottom the arms of Archbishop William Dalrymple Maclagan. On its west side is the See of York (ancient), on its east the See of York (modern). The inscription notes that the chapel, built by Archbishop Walter de Grey had suffered and was restored by Archbishop Maclagan in 1892.
Panelling	In oak with plain panels at the bottom and sixteenth-century type ones above, with a frieze of rounded strap-work with paterae, leaves and berries. Designed in 1920 by W. D. Caröe using Jacobean pews and good modern copies.
Piscina	In the south wall. In c. 1920 traces of a second altar and the original drain pipe for its piscina were found, and W. D. Caröe utilised the latter by turning a triple column there into a modern piscina.
Plate	In his will of 1683, Archbishop Richard Sterne left the chapel plate to the Dean and Chapter of York because the Minster plate had been stolen in 1676. A full account of the existing plate is kept at the Palace.
Reredos	At the west end; made in Oberammergau in 1898 and restored there later by Peter Rendel. It consists of a crucifixion on a round-headed panel with an enriched canopy; above it is 'IHS' and on either side two tiers of angels, looking inwards, with a scroll inscribed 'DOMINUS JESUS CHRISTUS'. At the bottom a central seat has a panelled front and kneeling angels at the sides, and on each sill is a seat like the others in the chapel.
Seating	The seating has shaped ends and fronts with open trefoiled arches on round shafts with moulded caps, bands and bases, and pierced quatrefoils in the spandrels. The fronts of the seats were repaired and cleaned in 1959-61 (Archbishop Ramsey).
Sedilia	Traces of three supporting brackets were found in 1920 on the east wall, and two new brackets were inserted by W. D. Caröe to produce a stone seat.
Standard lamps	Two, iron; designed by George Pace of York c. 1965, given by past members of the London School of Divinity to honour the Archbishop, Dr. Donald Coggan.

The Great Hall

The **great hall,** in the centre of the original medieval range and reached through the Gothick entrance-hall, is a noble room of the same size as the original thirteenth-century one, but it was rebuilt in the time of Archbishop Accepted Frewen (1660-4) and has a rich plaster ceiling with a bold contemporary frieze of early seventeenth-century character, which, like so many ceilings in the West Riding, was already old fashioned when built. The walls have, below the ornate frieze, a moulded cornice with dentils and beading, a moulded dado rail and moulded skirting. Above the dado is a series of tall panels formed by moulded and beaded surrounds based on a plain wood lining to the wall (first half of the eighteenth century).

The north wall has to the west of centre a doorway (page 61) with a moulded and eared surround; above it is a moulded and dentilled pediment and an entablature with a pulvinated frieze. At the top of the pediment is a pedestal for a bust. The door has six panels, fielded on both sides, and is of oak (exposed on the outer side). The strong simple hinges are of mid-eighteenth-century type and the door will be of the same date as the vanished staircase represented by some balusters, once in the undercroft. One would expect a second doorway, to the private sitting room, but this would have been blocked by the early nineteenth-century staircase down to the terrace.

The east wall has three large windows of the same height but varying in width (page 59). The first large window is of three lights with high-set transome and moulded mullions. The neat, oak, hung-sashes have large panes. The dado returns into the recess and drops in a curve on either side to a window sill. The top is plastered and the splayed jambs are covered with panels. In the lights above the mullions are the arms of Archbishops Frewen, Sterne and Dolben (all by Peckitt) in painted glass. The second window is a bay of the same form but with the addition of oblique lights and it has ornate plaster at the top and square set reveals with the same disposition of plain panels. The main members are of plaster and most of the glass is plate type with the arms of archbishops set in oblong leading. The arms in the top row are Lamplugh, Sharp, Dawes, Blackburne and Herring. The second row are Drummond (signed W. Peckitt), Markham and Longley. The third row Thomson, Magee (by J. W. Knowles) Maclagan (by Kempe) and Lang. The third window has two lights with arms at the top of Matthew, Hutton and Gilbert. The windows are not symmetrically disposed; the central one is framed by features in the ceiling but the lateral ones have outer sides under the ceiling beams and these will be the ones altered by Archbishop Gilbert (1757-61). The panels in the east wall vary in width.

In the west wall (page 59) is a chimney breast to the north of centre with three equal panels on each side, followed on the south by a doorway with a medium width panel over it and a further narrow one to the south again. The chimney breast frieze bears the arms of Archbishop Frewen (c. 1660). The fireplace itself is by Thomas Atkinson (1769) (page 61). It has a black marble slip in a grey-white veined marble surround; on either side a free-standing Roman–Doric column has a complete entablature of the same character as the modillioned cornice, with triglyphs on the frieze of the fireplace; a slight curve in the very crisp mouldings is like that of the doorcase mouldings. The polished steel grate has enriched frames to recessed panels and three round medallions at the top; there are urn forms on the side uprights to the railings and an elegant grille at the bottom. The doorway at the south end of the west wall is like that in the north wall but with no pediment, and it was inserted by Archbishop Magee in 1890-1. The heavy door is of oak and has a delicate Gothick treatment added on the other side; the oval brass handle is like that on the other door but the outer one is different.

To the west of centre in the south wall is a doorway like that at the other end. It led to the chapel and two steps still remain at the bottom, but it was blocked in 1890-1 and turned into a cupboard. The blocking is of elegant panels which may be some of the late seventeenth-century panelling of the hall. The hall floor is of medium-width pine planks (eighteenth-century).

The ceiling is of unequal bays formed by a spine beam and four cross beams running east to west, all with a lilac pattern on the soffit, moulded sides and pendants at the intersections. The first and fifth bays are narrow with deeply set oblong panels with moulded sides; the three centre bays have in each half a recessed panel with at the angles obliquely set sprays of fruit and flowers. Inside the panel is a large pendant and round it a circle of laurel leaves with seventeenth-century decoration, while on the panel soffit are obliquely set sprays of pomegranate. The third bay, aligned with the bay window is slightly more enriched. The pendants and corner sprays are similar but the centre is oval and at each cardinal point are two winged cherubs' heads (page 61). The fourth bay is smaller again and less ornate. The deep frieze (page 60) is made-up of about twelve different moulds with enrichment of masks, cherub's heads, lush flowers, festoons, birds and cartouches.

The Gallery

A large top lit passage (now known as the gallery) (page 62) to the west of the great hall is very interesting as it shows the rusticated brick exterior of the late seventeenth-century hall. It has a simple moulded dado rail and skirting; in the ceiling are three very effective circular light-wells with frosted glass at the top and a great moulded roll at the bottom. The brick work was exposed and the ceiling lighting installed during the time of Archbishop Coggan. In the north wall is a segmental headed doorway. The east wall rises to the full height of Archbishop Frewen's hall wall, in rusticated brick (as on the river front) with a moulded brick cornice at wall plate level. The first part of the wall is fully rusticated and then between two pilasters with moulded caps and bases there is a blocked window originally of three lights and two transomes; the reveals, mullions and transomes were hollow chamfered. The next part is a shallow chimney breast with on it a dado rail and skirting as elsewhere. To its south is another blocked window between pilasters and with two lights and two transomes. The west wall is of brick, almost certainly of early eighteenth-century date with cornice, dado rail and skirting; it curves inwards at the south end to a doorway to the entrance hall. The south wall is the rusticated wall of a porch which has been neatly adapted on the west side to form the jamb of the doorway, and to the east of it is a pilaster like those on the east wall. This area was a stairhall in the eighteenth century but the staircase was removed in 1965 for the bedrooms above the great hall had long since ceased to be used; the scar of the staircase still shows on the west wall (page 62).

The Private Sitting Room

The archbishop's private sitting room to the north of the hall, re-presents a medieval compartment of 1364-5 but the east and west walls have been rebuilt in the late seventeenth century. Then in 1891-2, in the time of Archbishop Maclagan, the 'boudoir' (later called the 'parlour') was reduced in length by four feet and a staircase put in to give access to the river through a doorway formed out of a window; a piece of the ceiling of the seventeenth-century room remains above the staircase (work probably done by James Demaine and Walter Brierley of York). The resultant well-proportioned room (page 63) is in an eighteenth-century style but the ceiling hints at an earlier date. It has four cased and plastered beams with a cove at the south end; three of the beams have an eighteenth-century cornice returning along them, but the fourth is of late seventeenth-century date and has on its soffit an enrichment of fruit and lilac-like leaves (as in the great hall) with a boss of berries at the centre. In the penultimate bay to the immediate north of the enriched beam, is a seventeenth-century decoration like a bow with laurel leaves and stylised sprays (page 63).

The north wall is featureless. In the east wall are three large windows each with Gothick intersecting tracery at the top; the hung-sashes are set in openings with plain segmental heads, square reveals and a recessed, panelled base; they are protected by similarly panelled shutters. In a shallow chimney breast towards the north end of the west wall is a fireplace with a modern Adamesque surround, moulded cornice and composition swags and festoons on the frieze; the slip is of veined green marble. Beyond a pilaster is a doorway with moulded surround and a door with six panels (fielded on the outside) and with brass knobs. The staircase of 1891, lit by a light high up in its east wall and taken out of the room at the south end, has in the ceiling a complete oval enrichment like that in the great hall, a moulded cornice on the south wall, and there are signs of a vanished dado and skirting.

The Gothick Block

The Gothick additions of 1766-9 by Thomas Atkinson to the west of the early main range consist of an entrance hall and drawing room with service rooms on each side.

The Entrance Hall

The entrance hall (pages 64 and 65) is an elegant room of five bays which has been effectively coloured (in blue and white by Archbishop Ramsey and later in terracotta and white by Archbishop Blanch). Each long wall (i.e. north and south) has five bays framed by vaulting shafts with foliated caps and moulded bases; while each bay has a doorway-like recess with four-centred head and moulded reveals. At the bottom is a bold skirting returning round the pilasters and into the recesses. Above each feature is an ogee gable with undulating crockets and a great elongated finial. In the spandrel are cusps with enriched points. A doorway to the gallery in the second bay of the north wall has an oak door with applied decoration in window form, with four-centred head and intersecting tracery; each major 'light' has two sub-lights, cinquefoiled and resting on a corbel, and there are paterae in each quatrefoiled spandrel formed; under a transome are cinquefoiled lights, similarly treated; the mullions have exquisite capitals. The door has a well shaped brass handle. There is a similar door in the fourth bay, to the drawing room. The south wall has similar door-ways, in the second bay to the chapel and in the third bay to a large room to the south-west. The oak carving is excellent.

The main entrance is in the west wall (page 64) and it consists of three two-centred archways, open to the ground. Between two free-standing piers is a doorway in the centre and on either side are great hung-sash windows; the top lights of these have open cusps and the upper sash has four panes but the lower one has eight. At the bottom of each window are two large brass knobs to lift the lower sashes or as attachments of blinds. Above the doorway is a fixed light like the others and of six panes containing the sixteenth-century arms of Archbishop Grindal (the oldest glass in the Palace repositioned for Archbishop Blanch by Peter Gibson of the Minster Glass Shop in 1975). The doors have large plate glass panels.

The east wall (page 64) has the same disposition but no glazing and it embodies attractive Gothick plasterwork. There are three recesses with splayed sides and flat back, and in the centre one is an oak door, enriched like the others, leading to the great hall. The plasterwork has delicate curvilinear decoration. The plaster vault has moulded ribs of flattened Perpendicular character and the foliated bosses are very bold. The triple-shafted wall ribs have boldly modelled capitals.

The Drawing Room

A doorway from the entrance hall leads to the **drawing room,** a large handsome room with excellent craftsmanship. It has a moulded and enriched cornice with a hollow containing an undulating cusped trail with Perpendicular type leaves. The dado rail is rather crude with mouldings that are not Gothic, and there is a moulded skirting. The room is panelled in two heights in plaster, and large oblong panels are set between tall narrow ones.

The ceiling (page 67) has an enriched lozenge grid and in each panel is a circle, with a rim of folded leaf, a shallow foliated pendant and curvilinear tracery. The moulded ribs have small paterae in hollows and each intersection has a shallow pendant. There is a fine glass chandelier hanging from the middle pendant and those to the north and south have pulleys for lamps. The features are all from one mould, unlike the diversity found in the great hall.

The north wall has a doorway (page 67) with two-centred head and continuous reveals under a modillioned and battlemented cornice. In each spandrel is an off-set shield in a double-cusped quatrefoil with daggers outside. The flattened rere-arch is enriched with a quatrefoil, paterae and two cinquefoiled daggers. The doorway is classical to the north and Gothick to the south, and there is an oblong panel above it on the drawing room side. Two doors are set in the thickness of the wall, that on the north side is square-headed and has fielded panels, but the heavy one to the drawing room has a two-centred head and is decorated with a window-form of six lights with intersecting tracery, with at the top a circle containing a double-cusped quatrefoil and foliated paterae; there is a deep transome, enriched with oblong quatrefoils, and cinquefoiled lights below. The door is furnished with an attractive foliated brass knob, brass lock and key. On the inner (wall) side of this door are flush panels.

In the centre of the east wall page 66 is a fireplace with marble surround and on either side a white marble pillar of four separate shafts, with a large enriched abacus, cornice and moulded base, all in one piece. In each case the demi-octagonal abacus returns as a cornice in white marble with paterae in a hollow and within this, under a band of quatrefoils with foliated cusps, is a white-marble, moulded, four-centred headed opening, set in variegated brown Sicilian marble. The iron back and grate are contemporary. The overmantel is a panel with a band of Gothick trellis under a cornice like that of the over-doors.

In the west wall (page 66) are three tall, hung-sash windows, each with four-centred head and heavy moulded surround and reveals that run down to the floor; above a band of flattened quatrefoils are working shutters with blind cinquefoiled lights alternating with quatrefoils with paterae set on squares, and the slightly splayed head is similarly enriched; the upper six-pane sashes have intersecting cusped tracery (late eighteenth-century) but the lower ones are of plate glass (nineteenth-century).

The south wall is like the north one in all respects including the doorway (page 67). The outside of the door to the entrance hall is of oak, but the painted Gothick inner side is of pinewood; a knob on the inside is foliated but one on the outside is a shaped eighteenth-century type.

Service Rooms to the North of the Gothick Block

To the north of the drawing room is a group of compartments of post medieval date which infill the area between the medieval main range, the late fifteenth-century north range and the additions of the eighteenth century; they provide access and services of various sorts.

To the west of the private sitting room a passage with plaster barrel vault gives access at its south end to the great hall, and to its west is a modern staircase rising to the first floor, and a water closet with very attractive coved-headed niches of Adamesque character. A large oblong hall to the south of the last (page 68) has a doorway on the east to the private sitting room; in the south wall on either side of a well-designed lift of 1891-2 made for Archbishop Magee, which reaches from the basement to the bedroom floor, is a doorway to the great hall and one to the gallery which is to the east of the drawing room. The gallery is the same length as the drawing room but presumably preceeded the Gothick work as it had an early eighteenth-century staircase in it. A doorway to the west led to a large room of 1766-9 which was altered by Archbishop Vernon Harcourt

(1807-47) into a billiard room and was lit by two lunette windows, now blocked. It was the archbishop's library in 1891, replacing the original one on the ground floor of the Atkinson block to the south west, and was fitted with two mahogany bookcases and another new one. It was a second drawing room in the time of Archbishop Maclagan (1891-1909) and was by then known as **Harcourt.** It was divided in 1972-3 into two rooms; the north one, used as a kitchen, has a window like those in the drawing room, and the south part, reached from the drawing room, forms a nice lofty anteroom with a moulded dado rail and skirting. The plain ceiling has a Gothick cornice with undulating Perpendicular leaves and a window as in the drawing room. To the west of Harcourt is an outside yard which provides the way down to a newly formed utility room (to the north of Harcourt) and to a passage added to the north range on its south side, and to steps down to the undercroft in the south-east corner. A room to the west of this kitchen, in the block added in *c.* 1650 by Colonel White and later called **Sterne,** was altered in *c.* 1920 by W. D. Caröe and has now (1972) been turned into a private entrance to the Archbishop's accommodation in the north range, by making a new doorway, of the same proportions as the window at first floor level, in the south wall, and a new opening in its east wall to the passage on the south side of the north range.

Service Room to the South

A large room to the south west, wholly within the range of 1766-9 and reached from the entrance hall, forms the access to the administrative offices. It was the library before 1891 and is now divided, to provide cloakrooms and a modern staircase to the secretariat. The ceiling has two cased beams and a bold cornice which carries round them but is lacking on the north. There is a moulded dado rail and skirting and the walls are panelled in two heights. The north wall has a doorway to the east of centre with four-centred head, continuous moulded surround and cusped spandrels. The heavy door in a pinewood frame has an oak face to the hall and flush mahogany veneer on its inner side. A large fireplace in the centre of the east wall has a veined white marble surround and a steel grate of *c.*1900. A doorway at the south end is modern. At the north end of the west wall is a window, as in the drawing room, with good armorial bearings in the glass of Archbishops Williams, Neile, Mountain and the See of York. There are two other similar windows, one of which has the arms of Archbishops Matthew, Hutton, Piers and the Royal Arms. This glass was moved here from the chapel in Archbishop Maclagan's time, and is by William Peckitt (1767).

The Upper Floors of the Main Range

Plan page 7 Upper Floor.

These consist of rooms over the chapel, the roof-space over the great hall, rooms above the private sitting room and rooms over the Gothick addition.

The **six rooms above the chapel,** built for Archbishop Vernon Harcourt (1807-47), which were made into two good sized rooms, a small room, a lobby and a passage in the time of Archbishop William Thomson (1862-90), were again altered in 1971-2 to give the archbishop a study, and to provide accommodation for the secretary and staff. A new entrance and staircase were made to the south of the main entrance to the state rooms. At the south-east corner is the **Archbishop's study,** a pleasant, well-fitted, modernised room with moulded cornice and skirting. The north and west walls are fitted with bookshelves from King Edward's room; there are two hung-sash windows in the east wall, each with pointed head, intersecting tracery and a simple roll on the angles. A doorway at the north end of the west wall has a modern surround and a mahogany door with six panels. In the south wall is a large three-light window with chamfered mullions and reveals and a high-set transome (late nineteenth-century). In the south-east corner is an obliquely set fireplace with moulded surround, moulded mantel shelf and a grate of c. 1900. A **lobby** on the outer side has similar features and the **chaplain's room** beyond has a similar cornice and doorway, plain east and west walls, a large window like that in the study, and the fireplace, obliquely set in the south-west corner, has a shaped frieze (c. 1900). From the outer lobby a staircase leads down to the first floor of the added Gothick range.

In the **roof space above the great hall** is a roof of three bays (seventeenth-century); it was intended to be hidden for the trusses have large, rough principals, crude collars of re-used wood, two purlins on either side and great ties with joists let into them, all of oak (page 69). There are also four inserted iron trusses with curved girders and longitudinal members, perhaps fitted by Sir Robert Smirke in c. 1840 when the roof was declared unsafe. In the eighteenth century three small rooms had been formed in this roof space with fireplaces and chimney breasts in the centre, and hung-sash windows on either side of each bay and also in the dormers on the east side. The rooms were ceiled at collar level, and the floor joists still remain, but the arrangements were spoilt when the iron trusses were fitted (page 69). The staircase from the upper rooms to the gallery was removed in 1965. Dr. William Thomson, Archbishop, built a water tower in the grounds in 1863 and it was connected to two cisterns fitted above the hall; but they were prone to freeze easily and were later removed.

Over the private sitting room a bedroom and sitting room of *c.*1750 have been formed. The **bedroom** has a cased beam in the roof and the floor has been fitted below tie-beam level. A door towards the east end of the north wall is screwed up. A hung-sash window in the east wall has a moulded surround, splayed reveals and plain panels down to the floor. There is a cupboard at the south end and in the west wall is a fireplace with a moulded cornice and surround. A doorway at the west end of the south wall has a moulded surround and a door of four panels (fielded on the one side) with a brass lock. The **sitting room** to the south has the same general characteristics with similar doorway and window, but with later hung-sashes and an eighteenth-century fireplace. There is a modern bathroom to the south.

In the **mid-eighteenth-century Atkinson addition** are; a steep narrow **staircase** leading down to the north range first floor corridor; the **assistant secretary's room** with original moulded dado and skirting, and an original window; a room used for filing cabinets with a similar Atkinson window; the **secretary's room** where the fittings are modern except for the original window; the waiting and reception room where a modern window replaces the vanished oriel; a **book store** where all the features are modern and the **lay chaplain's room** which has a fireplace with a Gothick surround.

North Range Ground Floor

Plan page 6.

The north range consists of a ground floor, first floor and attics.

The Ground floor is very complex. From east to west there are a great kitchen with lobbies and passages to the south of it; the Archbishop's dining room, an entrance hall to the archbishop's private appartments; a waiting room, a large room now used for Diocesan business, a passage and hall to the south, another kitchen, a staircase hall and cloakroom; a large room at the south-west corner, a room in the projecting block to the south of the last one, and a small one beyond.

The **kitchen,** built for Archbishop Rotherham at the north-east angle of the medieval main range *c.* 1480-1500, was later divided into two rooms called **Blackburne** (the assistant secretary's office) and **Roger** (the butler's pantry). It was rehabilitated in 1972 and was completed in its present form by 1976. It is a fine lofty room and has in the roof three large oak ceiling beams running north to south, chamfered and deeply scored for plaster. Against the north wall is a great projecting chimney breast of plastered red brick; it has a large opening with segmental ashlar head, and continuous, plain chamfered reveals with low-set stops; the stone has butt-ended tooling of late fifteenth-century type. The opening has kitchen fittings set against an inner wall (1976) (page 70). At the east end of this wall is a relatively deep cupboard of late eighteenth- or early nineteenth-century date. A new hung-sash window has been inserted and to the west of the chimney breast a mid-eighteenth-century hung-sash window has been fitted into a c. 1500 opening.

There is a large hung-sash window in the east wall with thin glazing bars and a moulded surround with square angle pieces (c. 1830). The shutters on either side have four panels and nice knobs. The west wall is of late medieval brick, now plastered over; a doorway to the south of centre driven through the medieval wall, has square reveals and a Gothic head and a modern six panelled door. The medieval brick south wall has several openings in it. The first is modern, but on the site of an older opening for the west jamb is of plain-chamfered ashlar, and high up on the east side is an old jamb stone. In 1976 it was turned into a hatch, on the outer side of which there is evidence for blockings of c. 1750 and 1800. The second opening is a doorway with splayed reveals, set against an earlier blocking of the original opening. On the south side it has a fine moulded surround with a hollow between two wave moulds and plain, low-set stops (early fourteenth-century). A tall third opening has splayed reveals and a square head, and within it is a broad lower doorway of c. 1840-50. The eighteenth-century type door has six panels, plain on one side and fielded on the other, but has been enlarged and is now wholly modern. The brick walling beyond is of the same date as a transverse arch here (c. 1480).

The **lobby** to the south and east of the kitchen has now become a small breakfast room by the insertion of modern walls, and, in another passage or lobby formed to its west, has in its north wall the jambs of a window, and a fine doorway of c. 1350. To the west again is a medieval transverse wall which is not on the line of the outer wall of the main house, but lines up with a chord wall in the undercroft; in this transverse wall is an opening with a four-centred head and a rere-arch rebated on the east side; on the west side the doorway has a four-centred moulded head with two hollows and a roll, deeply chamfered jambs with large pyramidal stops, and part of a moulded label set on leaves with, on its north end, a damaged heraldic stop of three stags for Archbishop Rotherham. The archway is set into another archway of the same date and running east to west. The second doorway has a moulded head likewise, and in the spandrel is an elegant man with long hair, a bonnet with a large feather, and two dogs leaping up at him (c. 1480) (page 70). The passage south wall contains old brick and at the east end is a blocked opening with an oblong light at the top. To the west again is a modern opening leading to a staircase of c. 1830. A **lobby** to the west of that complex has a floor of freestone flags with black marble insets, and doorways of various dates including the late fifteenth-century one already mentioned.

The **archbishop's private dining room** was formed for Archbishop Garbett (1942-56) (page 71). It has a small hollow chamfered cornice and a modern skirting. In the ceiling are two shallow stop-chamfered beams; there is no beam above the east wall and at the west end the beam has a chamfer on the east side only, proving that the west wall is medieval, although a curved support here is not. There is a modern herring-bone-wise parquet floor; a diagonal section in the north-east corner shows the position of the previous fireplace. In the centre of the east wall is a doorway with four-centred head and a simple surround with shallow rolls on each edge. The modern door is of eighteenth-century type. The north wall has two windows each with moulded surround, splayed jambs and, on each side, one small and three large panels with applied moulding (*c.* 1840). The hung-sashes have fairly heavy glazing bars (mid-eighteenth-century) but the windows were lowered in Dr. Ramsey's time (1956-61). A fireplace in the centre of the west wall was found by Dr. Garbett and it has a flattened head and square brick jambs with wide mortar joints (late fifteenth-century). On either side is a doorway of fifteenth-century type; the north one has crude fielding on the inside but the other one has correct fielded panels. Over the fireplace and set fairly high is a stone angel, with curly hair, good wings and a nice embroidered collar holding a shield of arms:– *Gules* on a pallium *argent* over an archiepiscopal cross, five crosses crosslet fitchées *sable* (York ancient) impaling *azure* three stags trippant *or* (Rotherham) (page 72). The south wall has at the east end a doorway like the others but with a modern door and a nineteenth-century brass knob (*c.* 1960). In the centre of the wall is a large square-headed, two-light window with shallow splays, freestone segmental headed lights without cusps, blind spandrels and on the inside rebates for shutters (*c.* 1500).

There is a small scullery to the north-west, then a room once a larder and remodelled in September 1972 as a cloak room, and to the west again is a staircase leading down to a disused cellar, formerly a boiler room, running westwards to the end of the range. Various passages and lobbies beyond have been remodelled recently and embody features of *c.* 1830; in the north wall of one of them is a large doorway of *c.* 1480, recently rediscovered (page 72); it has a flattened head, chamfered reveals and shallow, carved spandrels, one with a single rose and leaves and the other with a wild man and Perpendicular type leaves.

An **entrance hall to the archbishop's private apartments** was being formed in 1972 in a room called **Sterne** which was once a kitchen. This room was part of the seventeenth-century block built for Colonel White in the angle between the main range and the north range. The north wall of dark red brick had a plinth of magnesian limestone cut back at the bottom of the western half (*c.* 1480) and there were three blocked door-ways in it. On the east side is a large seventeenth-century chimney breast with modern blocking in the opening; a partition wall of mid-seventeenth-century date four feet six inches to its north was broken through in 1972 and a staircase removed, but it still remains above. To the south of the chimney breast was a relatively modern doorway. The west wall was of seventeenth-century brick and in it is a double hung-sash window in square reveals, with panelled shutters and thin glazing bars (nineteenth-century). The jambs of earlier windows were visible on either side of the upper half. The south wall is of the same brick and a blocked doorway was reopened in 1972. The replaced floor was formed on re-used medieval timbers laid on soil. The room has now been effectively modernised and plastered, and the above notes were made during the restoration work.

The room to the north, called **Markham,** was previously the lay chaplain's office and has now been turned into a waiting room. It is reached through a lobby at the west end of the archbishop's private apartments and from the new entrance hall. Its fittings are of *c.* 1830 and the fireplace against the east wall has moulded jambs, lintel and square angle pieces and a plain mantel shelf. It is in the north east angle of the block added in *c.* 1830, perhaps by Sir Robert Smirke.

To the west is a large living room once the archbishop's sitting room and now used as a general **Diocesan room** in which many committees meet regularly. It is a spacious and well-lit apartment, partly in the range of 1480 and partially in the addition to the garden front of *c.* 1830. In the south-east part is a large intruded block which is really a chimney breast of the late medieval range. The room has a moulded cornice with swirling fluting and a moulded skirting. In the north wall are three fine, large, hung-sash windows with moulded surrounds, splays with working shutters and panels with applied mouldings on a slight field (Regency; of Adamesque character but almost certainly by Sir Robert Smirke *c.* 1830). The east side of the room has a plain wall in the northern half and the remainder sets forward about nine feet. In the forward half of the wall and at the north end is a fireplace (page 73) with veined white marble surround, plain jambs and lintel and round moulded paterae as angle pieces; there is a slip and a shaped mantel shelf with a quarter-round edge. The grate is a very good one with rectangular sides, each with a gadrooned top and elegant enriched base, on the jambs are high, claw-footed pedestals with festoons, swags and paterae, and on an oval with a winged monster in it is a seated female holding a wreath; at the top is a medallion, festoon and swags and on each cheek-piece is a garlanded standard; the grate has reeded hollow sides and there is a marble hearth. The entrance doorway, with the same surround as the window and a six-panelled door with elegant oval brass handle, is at the south end of the west wall.

A doorway through the base of a medieval bay window to the south (formerly the archbishop's private entrance) leads to a hall and a kitchen once noted as the housemaids' closet and now called **Chad. A staircase**

hall which is paved with limestone flags and black marble lozenge insets, has a doorway in the north wall to the garden. The staircase (page 73) has a moulded mahogany rail, turned newel and square mahogany balusters with small rolls on the angles. The cantilevered pinewood treads have recessed panels on the soffits. Water closets in a cloakroom to the west of the stairs have delightful coved-headed niches with round back and Regency type panels to house the pedestals, and good washing facilities.

A badly lit room called **Musgrave** at the south-west corner and at the end of the range of 1480, was, in 1971, the secretary's office. It has early nineteenth-century fittings and on the north side a shallow chimney breast with a plain surround with jambs, lintel and square angle pieces (*c.* 1830) and with an overweening mantel shelf of *c.* 1900. At the east end is a nice composition of a large deep niche with segmental head and within the base four tiers of drawers surrounding a cupboard, all acting as a sideboard. On either side is a six-panelled door, each with moulded surround with moulded jambs, lintel and angle pieces; the north door is to a cupboard and the southern one is the entrance to the room. On the west side are two hung-sash windows together in a recess with fielded panels to splays and soffit and a window seat with horizontal fielded panels (late eighteenth-century).

A room to the south of the last called **Magee** and once the chaplain's sitting room is quite different from any other in the house and is a valuable example of Commonwealth decor (pages 74 and 75). It has a moulded and enriched cornice, moulded dado rail and skirting, all of good quality. It is panelled in two heights with a projecting moulded frame and recessed fielded panels. The north wall has a large doorway with continuous enriched surround, but the top is blocked and the six-panelled door is of Regency type as elsewhere. The doorway is of the type produced by the Etty family of York, as seen at one time at the Queen's Hotel, Micklegate, York and still at Bramham Park. A fireplace (page 75) in the east wall has a bolection-moulded surround of brown shelly marble with over it a wooden, enriched, bolection-moulded panel above which the cornice steps forward. Under the panel is an enriched cornice and an oblong recessed panel between two volutes. To the south of the fireplace, through a camouflaged doorway, is a small lofty cupboard, lined with plain panels and lit by a large hung-sash window with plain shutters (eighteenth-century). In the west wall the cornice steps out over two hung-sash windows together in a fielded panelled recess as in **Musgrave;** they replace an earlier window of the same width but with the sill at dado level. In the south wall is a partially disguised doorway with over it a fixed horizontal panel and the door has an eighteenth-century look. Through this doorway is an oblique passage with reveals of fielded panels.

A **study to the south of Magee** was enlarged by taking down a partition to include a useless inner room. It is lined with two heights of fielded panels with moulded cornice, dado and skirting (eighteenth-century). The entrance has a moulded surround and no door on the inner side. There is a hung-sash window in the east wall as before; the north and south walls are fully panelled and in the south-east angle is an obliquely set chimney breast with a nineteenth-century fireplace (page 75) with plain jambs, lintel and mantel shelf. Over it is a horizontal fielded panel, a simple moulded cornice and above again a large bolection-moulded panel.

North Range First Floor

The disposition of the first floor rooms is much the same as that on the ground floor and consists of the archbishop's bedroom and dressing room, five guest rooms, a large room divided into two, a long passage and bathrooms on the south side, a family room with passage to the south, a hall and staircase hall, a bathroom, and three rooms at the west end, of which two are in the seventeenth-century projecting block to the south-west. (Plan page 7.)

The room called **Toby Matthew** and once a guest's bedroom is now the **archbishop's bedroom** and is at the north east corner of the range of *c.* 1480. It had been modernised in *c.* 1830 but a hung-sash window in the north wall (page 76) has square reveals, heavy ovolo-moulded glazing bars and good crown glass in the twelve panes (early eighteenth-century). An oblique fireplace in the north-west corner is of *c.* 1830. In the east wall are two hung-sash windows placed together, with thin glazing bars and reveals with applied mouldings; each splayed jamb has five panels of which the upper parts are shutters, and there are three large panels of the same kind below the windows. A doorway at the south end with a moulded case, a door with six Adamesque panels and contemporary knob has now (1983) been blocked. A projection into the south-west corner of the room, with the entrance door in it, is the end of a large passage running along much of the range on its south side, giving access to various small service rooms, and in this passage area is a doorway of *c.* 1480 (page 76).

The **archbishop's dressing room,** called **Holgate** and previously a guest room, has doors and windows of *c.* 1830. The next room to the south, called **Zouche,** has a hung-sash window in the north wall, with glazing bars of average width and shutters with fielded panels (eighteenth-century); a fireplace in the east wall has a plain surround, mantel shelf, and a nice grate (early nineteenth-century). A doorway at the east end of the south wall is of the same date. The next guest room, called **Baynbridge,** is larger and the fittings, fireplace and window are all early nineteenth-century, as in a service room to the south of it. The next room, **Kempe,** also with early nineteenth-century fittings, has a cupboard in the south-east corner entered from the passage outside; the room is all within the late medieval range.

The sixth room from the north, called **Wolsey,** was considerably enlarged in the time of Archbishop Maclagan (1891-1909) by removing a gable projection, reducing the size of a lobby on the south side and sacrificing two small rooms and an attic. It was once the archbishop's dressing room but is now another guest room; it is strangely shaped for it is partially in the north-east angle of the added early nineteenth-century block on the garden front. Its cornice is enriched with pellets and there is a trabeation between the newer and older parts. The window in the north wall is of Adamesque type and larger than the others. A fireplace slightly oblique on the east side has a plain early nineteenth-century surround; the west wall is in two planes and a doorway in the south wall has Adamesque features, matches the window and has a contemporary brass knob.

The next room, called **Sharp,** formerly the archbishop's bedroom, has a moulded cornice and skirting. In the north wall are two fine large windows with moulded surrounds and slightly fielded shutters; the very large panes retain their crown glass and there are four vertical panels in the recess at the bottom; the enriched pelmets could be original ones of *c.*1830. Against the east wall is a very shallow broad chimney breast with a fireplace with Regency surround; it has moulded and reeded jambs and lintel, round paterae at the angles and an oblong panel as a keyblock; the mantel shelf has three reeds on the edge and is original. At the south end of the east wall is a Regency doorway with the same case as the windows and a door with six panels with applied mouldings and ornate Victorian finger plates. The west wall has a doorway at its south end with the same surround and an original felt-covered door. The south wall is plain.

The room to the west is as large as the last one, was called **King Edward's room** and later became the archbishop's study before this was moved to a room over the chapel. The cornice is ornate and has reeded panels between rows of pellets and with foliated paterae at intervals (page 76); it has moulded dado-rail and skirtings; the fireplace and the two windows with their pelmets are like those in **Sharp** and the east wall has a similar doorway at the south end with two good Victorian fingerplates. The name of the room may reflect a visit by Prince Edward and Princess Alexandra for on 11th August 1866 they signed the Visitors Book and they occupied a suite in the north range, consisting of a bedroom furnished in blue satin, a dressing room and a sitting room in red damask. The royal room was turned into a study in Archbishop Ramsey's time (1956-61) and its furniture was put into store. This study was fitted out with shelves then by Mr. Simpson the local builder. In Archbishop Coggan's time they were removed to the present study.

A room in the mid-seventeenth-century block to the south of **Kempe** and **Wolsey** and called **Rotherham** has served many purposes (recently the den and the television room) and its fittings are *c.*1800. Its south window was inserted by Demaine and Brierley for Archbishop Maclagan.

The **passage** continues to the west and has a big bay window, over the one below, with two hung-sash windows in the outer face and others, one pane wide, to the south-east and south-west. The north side of the passage has a fine series of cupboards of *c*.1830. A **hall** at the end of the passage has an exceptional coved and enriched rococo plaster ceiling (page 77) of the school of John Carr; it is within the medieval range and was formerly the roof of the original staircase, replaced when one was built to the north of it in *c*. 1830. This ceiling has sprays of foliage, flowers and plum-like fruits. The later staircase hall to the north of the last provides access to adjacent bathrooms and services.

A large bedroom called **Thoresby** in the medieval part at the north-west corner, has fittings of late eighteenth-century type with paired hung-sash windows, and another large bedroom, called **Thurstan** has an eighteenth-century moulded cornice and skirting, and a fireplace in the east wall has a bolection-moulded surround and a moulded mantel shelf. A bathroom in the part added in 1650 has eighteenth century decor and a fireplace in the south-east corner has a plain stone surround; the south wall has an early eighteenth-century hung-sash window with heavy ovolo-moulded glazing bars. In September 1978 these rooms were being fitted out as a flat for occupation by the houseman.

North Range Attics

Plan see page 7 Upper Rooms.

The attics in the north range fall into four groups. (a) A flat at the east end of the range and connected with the upper parts of the main range. (b) An unused loft. (c) An isolated room to the south of (b). (d) Rooms at the west end.

The first group includes a dining room in the north-east corner, a hall to the south of it with staircase and passages; a passage running east to west; a small kitchen and two bedrooms. The **room in the north-east corner** is formed within the roof and is of two bays with a roof truss cased in planks which looks early and could be of a different construction from the trusses of *c*. 1480 further west; otherwise the fittings are of *c*. 1850. A **hall** serving this complex, to the south, has a hung-sash window and a series of collars in the roof about six feet apart. A **staircase** here has a moulded mahogany rail, cut string, turned newels and plain, square balusters (early nineteenth-century) it rises from opposite the present kitchen in four flights with two half-landings and two landings. Passages here are of the nineteenth century and include contemporary cupboards. The remaining passage, kitchen and two bedrooms have visible roof trusses and are all relatively modern.

The **roof** in the centre of the north range is reached through an opening in the west wall of the flat. The roof is of two dates (page 78). The eastern half has two original trusses of oak with two chamfered purlins on either side. The truss towards the east end has principals and a cambered collar, all properly pegged; there are no braces, the members were not exposed and thus were not chamfered; the truss is numbered four (////). The second truss has principals, a cambered collar beam and fine arched braces; it would be the exposed truss of a tall first floor room open from thence to the roof. In this part of the roof two great, deal planks act as collars. Beyond this arch-braced truss the ceiling of the rooms below has been heightened and above it is a later roof in pinewood with at least four trusses of mid-eighteenth-century date (the date of the rococco staircase ceiling below). Each truss has a king post, with enlarged head and base resting on a collar, with struts to principals on either side; the purlins and rafters have been replaced.

At the centre and to the south of the north range is an isolated room, **Sandys,** above the mid-seventeenth-century block; to the east, in this loft running east to west, an oak collar at the centre, supporting purlins, has had its middle cut out and there are blocked mortices at each angle; there is a sliding-sash window in the west gable and small dormers to east and west.

There are three rooms at the west end, now forming part of the houseman's flat. The first, in a loft running east to west, has a purlin exposed on either side, chamfered and of good quality and just inside the east wall is a complete arch-braced medieval truss, covered with plaster; there is another truss with plastered collar above the west gable. In the north wall is a fireplace with a nice early nineteenth-century grate. There is a modern window in the west gable, a dormer in the south wall and in the centre of the south wall is an early eighteenth-century door with a large panel between two horizontal ones, fielded on the outside and plain within. A second room to the south and in a loft running east to west, has a dormer at the east end of the north wall; in the east gable is a nice simple fireplace with a grate signed 'Carron'; there are cupboards with eighteenth-century doors on either side of the fireplace; there is a simple casement window on the west and in the south wall is an early eighteenth-century door. The third room to the south again is in a loft running north to south, lit at the south end and with square oak rafters in the roof. These lofts were adapted for use in the late eighteenth century.

The Stables

The older stables, enlarged by Archbishop Richard Sterne (1664–83), stood on the south side of the entrance drive and to the east of the present gateway; they were pulled down in 1760.

It is known that Peter Atkinson (1725-1805) made extensive alterations at the Palace in 1761, being helped by Thomas Atkinson of York with his drawings (J. W. Knowles, MSS in York Reference Library p. 11). The present stables (page 79) were being built in 1763 for Archbishop Drummond (1761-76) almost certainly by Peter Atkinson, for his partnership with John Carr produced the peculiar stone rustication found here (see appendix II). The stables formed a complete quadrangle, but in 1923-4 W. D. Caröe pulled down the east side after a very full photographic record, and the central part was converted into two excellent houses. In 1967-8 the occupied part was altered and improved again and the remainder of the stables were demolished, except the Brewhouse Cottage which is occupied by the chaplain.

The remaining front is in an impressive Palladian style, in brick with stone dressings and a plain tile roof. In the centre is a high projecting feature with rusticated quoins, and over a segmental-headed carriage entrance with Gibbs-type reveals is a Venetian window in a round-headed recess intruding upwards into an open pediment. Above again, and constituting the centre of the façade, is a tall dovecote with the same rusticated quoins and under its round pediment is a thermal window of two orders. On either side is a range of two storeys and three bays; the eastern range has a small Gibbs-type doorway with a light over it and between two deep hung-sash windows; above a string are three smaller windows. The western range has two large carriage entrances as in the centre block and the upper part is like the eastern range. On the outer sides again the building projects fowards, with rusticated quoins, Gibbs-type carriage entrances and above are Palladian features in open pediments that are slightly higher than the central pediment, but not as high as the dovecote.

The Gateway

The gateway (front cover and page 79) forms an effective outer frame to the Palace and is the most familiar feature to the passer-by. It may have been built on the line of a medieval ditch on the west side of the manor.

In the autumn of 1763 the foundations were laid of a gateway and porter's lodge, which were finished in September 1765 and designed by Thomas Atkinson of York. It embodies a clock dated 1744 which has on it the name of Thomas Herring (Archbishop 1743-7). It was the first of the Gothick buildings by Thomas Atkinson in the Palace complex. In 1894 (Archbishop Maclagan 1891-1908) it was in such a ruinous condition that Mr. Hodgson Fowler, the Diocesan architect, removed the turret and stopped the clock. A wooden turret was put up in 1895 and the room above the entrance was fitted out as a museum and playroom. In 1978 it was proposed to put the turret on a moulded base and a new lead roof, to be held by copper nails and clips, which were designed by Norman Riley, M.A., Dip.Arch., A.R.I.B.A. The gateway was repaired and reroofed by Roach, an architect to the Church Commissioners, in 1978-9.

The gateway is an interesting hybrid of Classical and Gothick and is built of magnesian limestone with some brown stone. It is square in plan, has a chamfered plinth and is of two storeys consisting of the entrance gate and a room above it; at each corner there are buttresses at right angles, of three stages, with weatherings and a gable at the top, and at each angle is a square pinnacle with bold gargoyle and a crocketted spirelet topped with a bold finial. On the west side there is a large segmental-headed archway with continuous mouldings and at its head the Royal arms in a garter carved in shallow relief:– quarterly (1) England impaling Scotland (2) France (3) Ireland (4) Hanover with on an inescutcheon a crown. A moulded label has stops of the See of York ancient to the north and the See of York modern to the south. Wooden gates on the outer side have two leaves in oak with Perpendicular enrichment. The first floor is lit by a four-light window with chamfered intersecting tracery and a label with carved stops. Above the window and below a moulded and enriched cornice with small battlements forming a pediment, is a blue round clock-face with Roman numerals in gold.

The inner eastern face is much the same, including the clock in the pediment, but at the top of the carriage-way arch are the arms of the See of York (modern) impaling (1) & (4) Drummond and (2) & (3) Hay, for Robert Hay Drummond, Archbishop 1761-76. The label stops are mitres. The north and south sides are of plain ashlar in three stages, with a pediment at the top. The roof of lead holds a modern open turret with conical roof and a weathercock. The carving is very competent. On either side of the gateway is a low battlemented wall with an open four-centred archway in it.

Gardens

By 1255 the gardens and a fishpond had been made for Archbishop Walter de Grey (Close Rolls 1254–56, 100) and by c. 1480 the area to the north was called the Warren. The garden was laid out formally in c. 1700 at the expense of Archbishop Sharp (1691–1714). He planted a fine avenue of lime trees and made a summer house near the fishpond; he refers to the warren and a watermill upon it. In the second half of the eighteenth-century an interesting Gothick tower was built near Warren Pond. Thomas Halfpenny, the head gardener at Bishopthorpe, was a founder member of the Ancient Society of York Florists in 1765; he was probably responsible for the planting of Knavesmire wood in 1774 with its avenue of lime trees from the Palace to the old church at Dringhouses (see R.C.H.M. *City of York III* p.38). In 1785 Dr. Markham (Archbishop 1777-1807) built a pigeon house, a large ice-house, an exceedingly good and convenient pinery and a flued wall 181 feet in length. Archbishop Vernon Harcourt (1807-47) included the warren in the garden and built a bath-house near to the pond. The Italian garden facing the north front was formed for Archbishop Thomas Musgrave (1847-60) by W. A. Nesfield (1793-1881). There were alterations in the garden and the fishpond was drained by Dr. William Thomson (Archbishop 1862-90). The garden at the south end of the house, once containing buildings, was called Mulberry Court, though only one mulberry tree now remains.

The house and gardens were taken over by the Church Commissioners during the period of Archbishop Garbett (1942-56) and the gardens were brought in order and some new lime trees planted. In Archbishop Ramsey's time new trees were planted at the end to screen the crematorium. Doors were made in the wall by the mulberry garden, where the kitchens were removed in the time of Dr. Garbett. The river wall was repaired and Mr. H. A. Scarth, architect, and Stewart Strain, Mrs. Coggan's brother, redesigned the terrace. A fine account of the gardens by Mr. Strain is kept at the Palace. The large kitchen garden on the other side of the Bishopthorpe road is still retained but the land to the north was let to a farmer.

Archbishop and Mrs. Blanch (1974-83) restored the sluice which controls the water level of Warren Pond and cleaned up its environs so it is now a pleasant haven for wild life.

Appendix I

Brick Rustication (seventeenth-century). Archbishop Frewen's rebuilding of the great hall at Bishopthorpe was in brick and the wall surface has an uncommon form of rustication. There are not many examples in the country. (a) The Old House at Blandford, Dorset built in 1650-70 by a German doctor (R.C.H.M. *Dorset* III part I (1970) 26-27, plate 110). This may give a hint of origins, but the house is typically 'artizan' style in London. (b) A house which formerly stood on the river front at Gainsborough, Lincs. (c) In Yorkshire there is a house in one of the old alleys of Hull and (d) one by the west end of the Benedictine nunnery at Nun Monkton. (e) In the City of York 64-66 Clifton, a timber-framed house in the suburbs, injured in the Civil War, was rebuilt afterwards with an attractive façade of this kind (R.C.H.M. *City of York* IV (1975) p.66 & plate 85) and (f) there is a small stretch of similar walling in a passage off Lendal towards the river. (E. A. Gee, *Architecture of York* (York 1979) (R.C.H.M. *City of York* V (1981) 155a).

Appendix II

Rusticated Quoins in Ashlar (generally eighteenth-century). A distinctive form of quoins in good ashlar appears in the stables at Bishopthorpe Palace and is described and illustrated in R.C.H.M. *City of York* III (1972) p.lxxx and fig. 14. The earliest example known to the author was on Clarendon House in London, built for the Earl of Clarendon by Sir Roger Pratt in 1664 and demolished in 1683 (R. T. Gunther ed. *Sir Roger Pratt on Architecture* (Oxford 1928) p.137 & plate opposite p.138) (J. A. Gotch *The English Home* (London 1919) fig. 118). The rusticated quoins were used on the original house at Swinton Park, built in 1719 (Pevsner *West Riding Yorkshire* (1966) p.363), on a garden portico at Knowsley in Lancashire (1733-37) and at Wentworth Woodhouse, West Riding, where the outer pavilions were altered by John Carr of York (H. M. Colvin English Architects (London 1954) p.124). John Carr particularly liked this form of rustication and he and his partner Peter Atkinson I who built these stables at Bishopthorpe, are associated with the following houses which all show it:– Newburgh Priory (North Riding) range to the left of the stables; Samuel Waud's house (1745) near Clifford's Tower, York (demolished); 39-45 Bootham, York (1747-8); Micklegate House, York (1752); Peasholme House, York (1752); Arncliffe Hall, North Riding, (1753) (Christopher Hussey, *Country Life* 25th Dec., 1920) (T. Whellan, *City of York and the North Riding* (Beverley 1859) II p.734); 53-55 Micklegate, York (*c.* 1755); Garforth House, Micklegate, York (1757). There are quoins of this type at Masham, Yorkshire and at Stamford (Lincs.).

Appendix III

Bishopthorpe Gothick and Strawberry Hill. Frances, Lady Waldegrave (1821-79) was concerned with Strawberry Hill, Middlesex in 1856-7 and constructed a new wing there in 1860-2, which has a lot of affinities with the Gothick work at Bishopthorpe. She married John Waldegrave, and afterwards his brother George, 7th Earl Waldegrave and finally Chichester Fortescue, but her third husband, George Granville Vernon Harcourt, was the son of Archbishop Vernon Harcourt and it was through him that she knew and copied the carving at Bishopthorpe. Her carver, Plows, was probably a Yorkshire man (cf. J. M. Mordaunt Crook, *Strawberry Hill Revisited,* Country Life 21st June 1973 pp. 1794-1796).

Manuscript Sources

Bishopthorpe I. By Archbishop Sharp, now bound and kept in the Borthwick Institute, York.

Bishopthorpe II. By Archbishop Sharp, dated 1693-4; as above. (These are chiefly concerned with rentals and Diocesan affairs.).

Bishopthorpe III. Kept at Bishopthorpe. Bound in full leather and entitled ARCHIVES OF THE SEE OF YORK. This was started by Archbishop Thomas Longley (translated from Durham to York 1860 and to Canterbury 1862). On p.43 he, as Archbishop of Canterbury and writing on 28th November 1863, leaves 'this book for future Archbishops to continue with items about Bishopthorpe'.

It continues with (a) notes written by Augusta Maclagan in 1893 from information supplied by Mrs. Thomson, widow of Archbishop William Thomson (1862-1890). (b) Notes by Mrs. Maclagan for the period of Archbishop William Connor Magee (1890-91). (c) Notes by Mrs. Maclagan for works in the time of Archbishop William Dalrymple Maclagan (1891-1908) (copied into the book by Rev. Wilfred Parker, chaplain to Archbishop Cosmo Gordon Lang). (d) Notes written in 1945 by Frances Temple, widow of Archbishop William Temple (1929-42). (e) Typed notes by Archbishop William Garbett (1942-53). (f) Notes by Mrs. Ramsey, wife of Archbishop Michael Ramsey (1956-61). (g) Typed list of alterations supplied by Mrs. Jean Coggan, wife of Archbishop Donald Coggan (1961-74).

Bishopthorpe IV. Kept at Bishopthorpe. Small book bound in green leather and lined gold, containing extra notes by Mrs. Maclagan. 'I am not the right person to insert in Archbishop Longley's "Archives of the See of York" the alterations and improvements made in the house after 1891, therefore I make this private book for the information and guidance of those who come after us, knowing how much we have regretted the absence of any continuous record of the various changes which have been made in past ages.' Augusta Maclagan.

Author's note: Many details about later alterations have been gleaned from Bishopthorpe III & IV, but as these manuscripts are not available for public inspection no specific references have been given in the architectural description.

Masons' Marks I

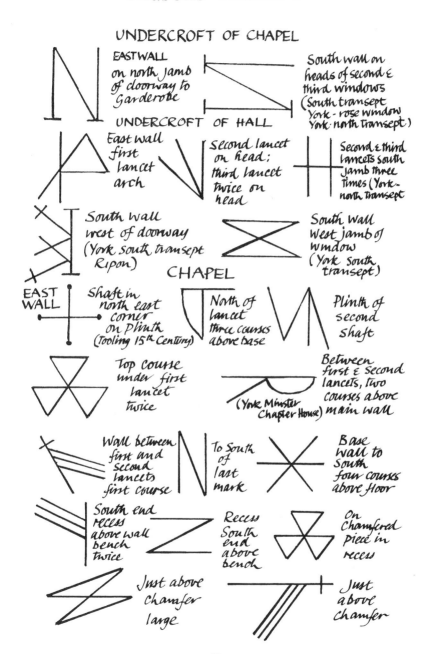

UNDERCROFT OF CHAPEL

EAST WALL
on north jamb
of doorway to
Garderobe

South wall on
heads of second &
third windows
(South transept
York - rose window
York north Transept)

UNDERCROFT OF HALL

East wall
first
lancet
arch

Second lancet
on head;
third lancet
twice on
head

Second & third
lancets south
jamb three
times (York-
north Transept

South wall
west of doorway
(York south transept
Ripon)

South Wall
West jamb of
window
(York south
transept)

CHAPEL

EAST
WALL

Shaft in
north east
corner
on Plinth
(Tooling 15th Century)

North of
lancet
three courses
above base

Plinth of
second
shaft

Top course
under first
lancet
twice

Between
first & second
lancets, two
courses above
main wall
(York Minster
Chapter House)

Wall between
first and
second
lancets
first course

To South
of
last
mark

Base
wall to
South
four courses
above floor

South end
recess
above wall
bench
twice

Recess
South
end
above
bench

On
Chamfered
piece in
recess

Just above
chamfer
large

Just
above
chamfer

45

Masons' Marks II

CHAPEL

NORTH WALL

first half bay six courses above bench

second recess (York South transept)

third recess pilaster to West near bottom

third recess seven courses above bench (Ripon north transept)

fourth recess; and under first lancet, South wall

last recess

SOUTH WALL

first bay in recess (York South transept)

first lancet under window (York South transept) Also in South recess

second recess second course

second recess first course

second recess fifth course (York South transept)

second recess third course third lancet on pilaster to West

third recess two courses above panelling

fourth recess one course above panelling

fourth recess first course Also in hall undercroft

fourth recess first & second courses (York south transept rose window; York north transept

fourth recess second course

fourth lancet in E jamb

fifth recess twice

fifth lancet

WEST WALL

Second shaft plinth five courses above bench

Second shaft (N. transept & S. transept York)

fifth shaft third & fifth courses

Sixth shaft first & fifth courses

46

Index

S. end of range 1766-9 with modern staircase and doorway; S. wall of chapel 1241-50; upper storey 1835

E. wall of chapel, garderobe and newel stair; lancets by Ewan Christian 1892

Undercroft of c.1250 and over it the hall of 1662 with windows altered in 1760; later gables

Rooms of 1365 and additions of c.1480, both refenestrated

Eastern half c.1480. Note diaper pattern and contemporary chimney heightened later

Western half, probably added by Sir Robert Smirke c.1835

W. end of N. range 1480 with later△
windows

E. face of S.W. block with medieval ▷
chimney breast and additions by
Colonel White c.1650

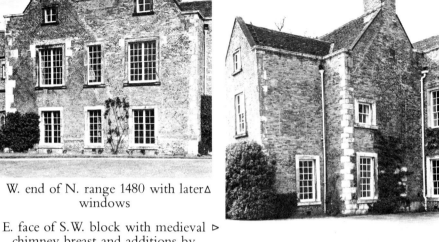

S. side of N. range with blocks added by Colonel White c.1650

GOTHICK FRONT 1766-9

The new front of the Archbishop of York's Palace at Bishopthorpe – 1769

Present front; the oriel has been removed

S. end of great hall undercroft, doorway of *c.* 1830; original doorway to newel stair; undercroft of chapel beyond.

Undercroft of great hall looking S.

Undercroft of great hall; complete lancet with 17th century blocking.

Wine cellar E. wall; rere-arches of 13th century lancets blocked in the 17th century.

Great hall undercroft, W. wall; base of hall fireplace of 17th century re-using a rere-arch of *c.* 1250.

Undercroft under private sitting-room; remodelled window in E. wall with rere-arch of 1364-5.

CHAPEL c.1250

Looking N.E.; lancets of 1892

Looking S.W.; lancets original but early W. window blocked in 1766-9
and the Oberammergau carving fitted in 1898

GREAT HALL

To N.W.; magnificent ceiling 1662 and fireplace by Thomas Atkinson 1766-9

To S.E.; windows remodelled later. Note the heraldic glass

N. end

Above fireplace with arms of Archbishop Frewen

S. end

Ceiling panel with cherubs' heads

Ceiling panel

Fireplace by Thomas Atkinson 1766-9
with portrait of Archbishop Frewen

Early 18th century doorway at N. end

Looking N.W.; shadow of 18th century staircase on wall

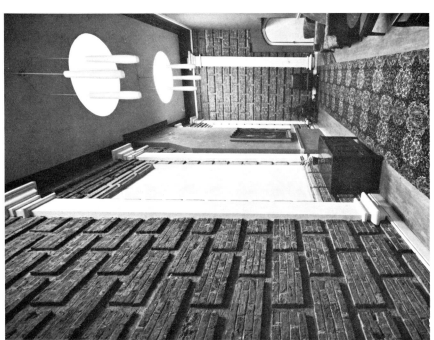

Looking S.E.; rustication 1662 of outside of hall and porch

PRIVATE SITTING ROOM

General view; room of 1364-5 remodelled in the 18th century.

17th century ceiling in the western bay.

ENTRANCE HALL 1766-9

Looking N.E.; elegant plaster decoration

Looking S.W.; entrance and plaster vault

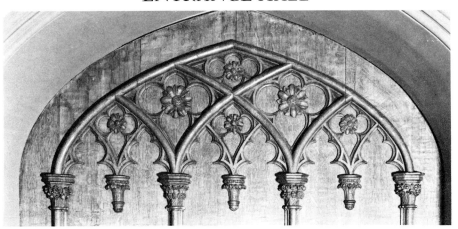

S. wall; door to Secretariat staircase.

N. wall; door to drawing room.

E. wall; door to great hall.

DRAWING ROOM 1766-9

Looking N.E.; fireplace with surround of coloured marble and original fittings

Looking S.W.; bottom sashes of windows 19th century plate glass.
Note Gateway

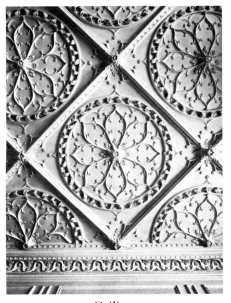

Ceiling

N. doorway with doors varying to suit adjoining rooms

S. doorway of painted pine in drawing room

Same doorway with oak carving to entrance hall

HARCOURT SQUARE

Lift made for Archbishop Magee 1891-2; door to Harcourt (Archbishop Temple 1929-42); glazed doorway to gallery.

Chest mentioned in inventory of 1628.

17th century roof principals, collar and purlins *c*. 1660; note window to removed bedroom.

Iron truss of *c*. 1840; bedroom fireplace.

Blackburn; kitchen fireplace; late 15th. century.

Carving of man and dogs
c. 1480.

Arms of Archbishop
Rotherham *c.* 1480.

Archbishop's dining room looking S.W.

Archbishop's dining room looking S.E.

See of York (ancient)
impaling Rotherham *c.* 1480
in dining room.

Window *c.* 1480 S. wall of
dining room.

Doorway of *c.* 1480 S.W. of
dining room.

Fireplace in Diocesan room.

Staircase *c.* 1830 near
Chad.

Passage to W. end of the
range with (Smirke) details.

NORTH RANGE – GROUND FLOOR
MIDDLE 17th CENTURY

Magee; interior looking N.W.

Magee; interior looking S.E.

Magee; cornice and panelling.

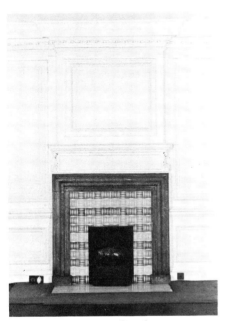

Magee; fireplace.

Fireplace in S. room of
S.W. block.

Toby Matthew; window
in Archbishop's bedroom.

Doorway of *c.* 1480 to S. of
Toby Matthew.

King Edward's room;
doorway.

King Edward's room;
cornice *c.* 1835.

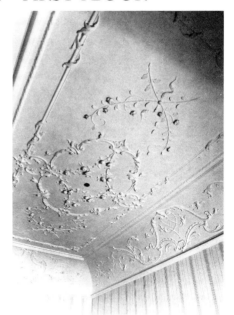

S. of **King Edward's room;** ceiling over vanished staircase, 18th century.

Truss at E. end *c.* 1480 with principals and collars but no braces; chamfered purlins.

Principals, cambered collar and chamfered purlins and arched braces *c.* 1480.

Early 18th century roof trusses; softwood king-post with enlarged head and base; principals pegged into head; struts and purlins.

CLASSICAL STABLES and GOTHICK GATE

Remaining range of stables by Peter Atkinson 1761-3. Note the peculiar rustication and the dovecote

Inside of gateway by Thomas Atkinson 1763-5. Renewed turret

RIVER FRONT

Kitchen wing in Mulberry Court demolished 1952.
Photo: Catcheside, York.

View across the river 1982.   Photo: J. Arthur Dixon.